T0146131

Exploring the Feasibility and Utility of
Machine Learning-Assisted Command and Control

Volume 2, Supporting Technical Analysis

MATTHEW WALSH, LANCE MENTHE, EDWARD GEIST,
ERIC HASTINGS, JOSHUA KERRIGAN, JASMIN LÉVEILLÉ,
JOSHUA MARGOLIS, NICHOLAS MARTIN, BRIAN P. DONNELLY

Prepared for the Department of the Air Force
Approved for public release; distribution unlimited

 PROJECT AIR FORCE

For more information on this publication, visit **www.rand.org/t/RRA263-2**.

About RAND

The RAND Corporation is a research organization that develops solutions to public policy challenges to help make communities throughout the world safer and more secure, healthier and more prosperous. RAND is nonprofit, nonpartisan, and committed to the public interest. To learn more about RAND, visit www.rand.org.

Research Integrity

Our mission to help improve policy and decisionmaking through research and analysis is enabled through our core values of quality and objectivity and our unwavering commitment to the highest level of integrity and ethical behavior. To help ensure our research and analysis are rigorous, objective, and nonpartisan, we subject our research publications to a robust and exacting quality-assurance process; avoid both the appearance and reality of financial and other conflicts of interest through staff training, project screening, and a policy of mandatory disclosure; and pursue transparency in our research engagements through our commitment to the open publication of our research findings and recommendations, disclosure of the source of funding of published research, and policies to ensure intellectual independence. For more information, visit www.rand.org/about/principles.

RAND's publications do not necessarily reflect the opinions of its research clients and sponsors.

Published by the RAND Corporation, Santa Monica, Calif.
© 2021 RAND Corporation
RAND® is a registered trademark.

Library of Congress Cataloging-in-Publication Data is available for this publication.

ISBN: 978-1-9774-0710-8

Cover: Tech. Sgt. R.J. Biermann/U.S. Air Force; Siarhei/Adobe Stock.

Preface

Recent high-profile demonstrations of artificial intelligence (AI) systems achieving superhuman performance on increasingly complex games along with successful commercial applications of related technology raise the questions of whether and how the U.S. Air Force can use AI for military planning and command and control (C2). The potential benefits of applying AI to C2 include greater decision speed, increased capacity to deal with the heterogeneity and volume of data, enhanced planning and execution dynamism, improved ability to synchronize multimodal effects, and more efficient use of human capital. Together, the technology push prompted by recent breakthroughs in AI and the market pull arising from emerging C2 needs have prompted the Air Force and the Department of Defense (DoD) to identify AI as a strategic asset.

In 2019, the Air Force Research Laboratory, Information Directorate (AFRL/RI) asked RAND Project AIR FORCE (PAF) to examine and recommend opportunities for applying AI to Air Force C2. The research project Exploring the Near-Term Feasibility and Utility of Machine Learning-Assisted Operational Planning was conducted in PAF's Force Modernization program to address this question. A second project was conducted in parallel to examine the separate but related topic of complexity imposition. This report presents the primary result of the study on AI: an analytical framework for understanding the suitability of a particular AI system for a given C2 problem and for evaluating the AI system when applied to the problem. We demonstrate the analytical framework with three technical case studies focused on master air attack planning, sensor management, and personnel recovery (PR).

The C2 processes examined in these case studies are central to current and future C2 concepts of operation, and they exemplify the range of characteristics that make C2 problems so challenging.

RAND Project AIR FORCE

RAND Project AIR FORCE (PAF), a division of the RAND Corporation, is the Department of the Air Force's (DAF's) federally funded research and development center for studies and analyses, supporting both the United States Air Force and the United States Space Force. PAF provides DAF with independent analyses of policy alternatives affecting the development, employment, combat readiness, and support of current and future air, space, and cyber forces. Research is conducted in four programs: Strategy and Doctrine; Force Modernization and Employment; Manpower, Personnel, and Training; and Resource Management. The research reported here was prepared under contract FA7014-16-D-1000.

Additional information about PAF is available on our website: www.rand.org/paf/

This report documents work originally shared with DAF on March 11, 2020. The draft report, issued on April 14, 2020, was reviewed by formal peer reviewers and DAF subject-matter experts.

Contents

Figures

Tables

Acknowledgments

We would like to thank our sponsor, Jack Blackhurst (Air Force Research Laboratory executive director), and our action officers, Nate Gemelli and Lee Seversky (Air Force Research Laboratory, Information Directorate [AFRL/RI]), for their help in shaping and performing this study. We would also like to thank Mark Linderman, Julie Brichacek, and Rick Metzger (AFRL/RI) for their valuable input during the study.

We are deeply appreciative of the assistance with data collection we received from many personnel, including Lt Col Dennis Borrman and Lt Col Jason Chambers (2020 RAND Air Force Fellows Program), LTC David Spencer and MAJ Ian Fleischmann (2020 Arroyo Army Fellows Program). We are also appreciative of the time that so many analysts and other personnel dedicated to participating in the expert panel.

Finally, we thank the many RAND colleagues who helped us with work. Principally, but not exclusively, we thank Michael Bohnert, Jim Chow, Henry Hargrove, Libby May, and Yuliya Shokh.

Abbreviations

A3C	Asynchronous Advantage Actor-Critic
AI	artificial intelligence
API	application programming interface
ASO	Air Surveillance Officer
ATO	Air Tasking Order
AWACS	Airborne Warning and Control System
C2	command and control
CL-ATR	closed-loop automatic target recognition
COA	course of action
COI	Critical Operational Issues
DARPA	Defense Advanced Research Projects Agency
DNN	deep neural network
DoD	Department of Defense
DRL	deep reinforcement learning
GH	greedy heuristic
IP	Isolated Personnel
ISR	intelligence, surveillance, and reconnaissance

IW	iterated-width
MAAP	master air attack plan
MCTS	Monte Carlo tree search
MIP	mixed integer program
ML	machine learning
MoE	measures of effectiveness
MoP	measures of performance
MoS	measures of suitability
NSTC	National Science and Technology Council
PAF	Project AIR FORCE
PR	personnel recovery
RL	reinforcement learning
SME	subject-matter expert
T&E	test and evaluation
TOS	time on station
V&V	verification and validation

CHAPTER ONE

Analysis of Problem Characteristics

Definitions

In Volume 1, we defined a taxonomy of ten command and control (C2) problem characteristics grouped into four categories. The *temporality* grouping comprises characteristics related to time. The first of these, *operational tempo*, is defined as the rate at which operations must be planned, replanned, and executed. This is not a generalized descriptor, such as "low" or "high," but rather a rate, such as "once every few days" or "within four hours or less." For example, an operation might require 12 hours to plan and an additional 24 hours to execute. The second characteristic, *rate of environment change*, is defined as how long it takes for the context to evolve from those previously encountered, rendering past tactics and learning outdated. While in many cases we can only know this imperfectly at best in advance, reasonable guesses as to low and high estimates can be made and used to guide planning. For instance, we could expect knowledge about the environmental context to remain valid for at least two weeks but probably not for more than a month with a high degree of confidence.

The *complexity* grouping includes two characteristics related to how difficult a problem is to solve, as well as the possible means of solving it.[1] The first of these, *problem complexity*, is meant to be analogous

---

[1] The notion of complexity here is distinct from complexity imposition through the use of multidomain effects—a C2 process that takes place in one domain can nonetheless have high complexity. Operating in multiple domains would tend to increase problem complexity, however.

to—and in rare cases equivalent to—computational complexity as studied in theoretical computer science. While computer scientists most commonly study the worst-case complexity of rigorously specified problems, in defense applications we tend to care more about the average-case complexity of problems. The problem complexity characteristic, therefore, tries to capture the resources required, in the abstract, to solve the problem in the average case to ensure the necessary degree of performance. This defines a limit bounding the performance of any algorithm or architecture on that problem. In many cases this limit will be specified relative to the size of the problem instance, for example, the available number of states and actions. The *reducibility* characteristic, by contrast, is the degree to which a problem can be decomposed into independent subproblems. For instance, if a task can be broken into two or more subtasks that can be solved by the same number of people or computers working in isolation from one another, then it is reducible.

The five characteristics included in the *quality of information* grouping aim to capture knowledge-related aspects of the problem. The first of these, *data availability*, describes the quantity, quality, and representativeness of data available for training and testing. Here, quantity, quality, and representativeness can be independent of each other. For instance, it is conceivable that one might have a simulator that can create an unlimited quantity of high-quality samples that represent only a small part of the possibility space or a limited quantity of low-quality samples that form a representative sample of the real-world distribution. *Environmental clutter/noise* aims to capture whether signals of interest are contaminated by signals from other potentially unknown and random processes. This characteristic is broadly analogous to the concepts of signal-to-noise ratio and false-alarm detection rate, although in some instances it cannot be measured in these terms. *Stochasticity of action outcomes* describes whether, and to what degree, the immediate effects of actions are predictable. If actions have randomized effects, even taking what is perceived to be the "optimal" move can sometimes result in an unfavorable outcome. *Clarity of goals and utility* is the extent to which the values of outcomes delivered during and at the end of a task are known and quantifiable. If payoffs include a randomized element that follows a known probability distribution, this characteristic is less than it would have been if those payoffs were deterministic and perfectly known. The critical *incompleteness of information* characteristic embodies many types of knowledge-quality problems that are difficult to quantify, for example, how much is known about the state of the environment and about the adversary's goals and intent. If the full extent of the environment is unknown and unexplored and the adversary's preferences are unknown, then only incomplete information is available, and many standard artificial intelligence (AI) methods for planning and game play will be inapplicable.

The *importance* grouping includes just a single problem characteristic—*operational risks and benefits*. This characteristic encompasses value judgments and is defined as the potential for the outcome to include the loss of something of value, or the advantage or profit gained. The operational risks and benefits characteristic can also encompass more than just straightforward utility calculations: in military use cases, the trade-offs are often between dissimilar and difficult-to-compare commodities, such as blood and treasure. There are also occasions when certain outcomes or choices must be excluded for reasons of law, custom, ethics, or decency. Responsible officials need to make these types of judgment calls about the "trade space" between operational risks and benefits; these judgment calls then enable analysis of whether potential solutions should be considered and how promising they appear.

Structured Interview Protocols

While the problem characteristics may seem intuitive, determining whether they are present in a problem may be challenging. Some characteristics can be formally defined, but others are of indeterminate formality. Of those that can be formally defined, some, such as operational tempo, may require only a single value for a well-defined task (e.g., blitz play in chess) but a dynamic range of values for a real-world task. Though the problem characteristics have technical definitions, Air Force operators will be more familiar with their everyday meanings.

To assist in this process, we created a structured interview protocol to enable scoring of problem characteristics for C2 processes with subject-matter experts (SMEs). The protocol is rooted in cognitive task analysis—a set of tools for identifying task demands and the cognitive skills needed to perform a task.[2] For each problem characteristic, SMEs were asked to reflect on their assigned C2 role and to provide examples.[3] SMEs were then shown a response scale with numerical ratings ranging from 0 (*not present*) to 4 (*present to a large extent*). The response scale contained definitions and examples for each rating that were specific to the problem characteristic. Based on the given definitions, SMEs were asked to assign a numerical rating to the problem characteristic for their assigned C2 role. Rating scales were developed for each characteristic. As an example, Table 1.1 presents the rating scale for one problem characteristic, operational tempo.[4]

Application to Specific Games and Command and Control Processes

Using the problem taxonomy and the structured interview protocol, we analyzed ten games and ten C2 processes. The results are summarized in Volume 1. The games are representative of those used for

---

[2] B. Crandall, G. Klein, and R. R. Hoffman, *Working Minds: A Practitioner's Guide to Cognitive Task Analysis*, Cambridge, Mass.: MIT Press, 2006.

[3] The use of examples relates to the critical decision method, in which a subject-matter expert retrieves past challenging experiences. Robert R. Hoffman, Beth Crandall, and Nigel Shadbolt, "Use of the Critical Decision Method to Elicit Expert Knowledge: A Case Study in the Methodology of Cognitive Task Analysis," *Human Factors*, Vol. 40, No. 2, 1998.

[4] The highest level of operational tempo also encompasses processes that take place on the timescale of microseconds and that would require machine-to-machine actions, like cyber attack, detection, and mitigation.

Table 1.1
Sample Rating Scale for Operational Tempo

Operational Tempo
The rate at which operations must be planned, replanned, and executed

Rating	Definition	Example
0	Responses are needed on the timescale of **weeks or longer**.	*The division is planning routine resupply missions that occur on a biweekly basis.*
1	Responses are needed on the timescale of **days**.	*The planning cycle used to create an Air Tasking Order (ATO) takes several days to complete.*
2	Responses are needed on the timescale of **hours**.	*The cell is planning a rescue mission. The mission must be ready within hours.*
3	Responses are needed on the timescale of **minutes**.	*The planner is responsible for air and missile defense. He must coordinate and execute a defensive response within minutes of threat detection.*
4	Responses are needed on the timescale of **seconds or less**.	*The pilot is maneuvering an aircraft. He needs to respond to the moment-by-moment behaviors of the adversary.*

AI test beds; the C2 processes, in turn, are representative of the military targets of transition for AI. The C2 problems were selected to achieve breadth of coverage across services, across command echelons, and across stages of the air tasking cycle (and joint operation planning more generally). The games are described in Table 1.2; the C2 problems, in Table 1.3.

To increase the validity and reliability of ratings, the structured interview protocol and analyses used the set of anchored scales developed for the ten problem characteristics. Members of the project team had experience with each of the games and AI test beds listed in Table 1.2. For each game, two members of the project team rated the ten problem characteristics based on experience and a review of available documentation. All ratings given by team members matched or were adjacent to one another. Disagreements were discussed and resolved.

Table 1.2
Description of Games

Example	Type	Description
Tic-tac-toe	Two-player turn-based game	Game is played on a three-by-three board. Goal is to place marks on three adjacent cells.
Tetris	Single-player real-time strategy game	Tile-matching puzzle game that involves fitting pieces to form complete rows.
Checkers	Two-player turn-based game	Game is played on an eight-by-eight board. Goal is to capture all of opponent's pieces by jumping over them.
Chess	Two-player turn-based game	Game is played on an eight-by-eight board. Goal is to place opponent's king under inescapable threat of capture (i.e., checkmate).
Go	Two-player turn-based game	Game is played on a nineteen-by-nineteen board. Goal is to surround more territory (cells) than opponent.
Texas Hold'em	Multiplayer turn-based game	Card game that involves forming strongest five-card hand from two hold cards and five community cards.
CartPole-v1	AI test bed	Continuous control task that involves keeping pole attached to an unactuated joint on a cart upright by moving the cart along a frictionless track.
HalfCheetah-v2	AI test bed	Continuous control task that involves teaching a physics-based two-legged agent (HalfCheetah) to run.
Bridge	Multiplayer turn-based game	Four-player game in which two teams of two players attempt to predict and win a set number of tricks.
StarCraft II	Single- or multiplayer real-time strategy game	Real-time strategy game that involves gathering resources, building units, and attacking competing players.

Table 1.3
Description of Command and Control Processes

Example	Service	Description
Intelligence preparation of the battlefield	Army	Method for collecting, organizing, and processing intelligence to provide timely, accurate, and relevant intelligence to military decisionmaking process.
Master air attack plan (MAAP)	Air Force	Create time-phased air and space scheme of maneuver for a given ATO period.
Nuclear retargeting	Air Force	Conduct adaptive planning to destroy as many adversary offensive nuclear forces as possible before they can be launched.
Operational assessment	Air Force	Evaluate the effectiveness of daily air, space, and information/nonkinetic operation planning and execution.
Personnel recovery: locate and authenticate	Air Force	Determine location of isolated personnel and authenticate their identity.
Reallocating intelligence, surveillance, and reconnaissance (ISR) assets	Air Force	Receiving requests for new ISR and dynamically replanning for and servicing requests.
Sensor management	Air Force	Process of controlling sensors aboard an Airborne Warning and Control System (AWACS) to detect, track, and identify airborne vehicles that may affect friendly operations.
Military decisionmaking process	Army	Multistep planning process for military decisionmaking at echelons with a command staff.
Tomahawk planning	Navy	Planning process surrounding launch of Tomahawk Land Attack Missile to ensure that it reaches its target at the prescribed time.
Troop leading procedures	Army	Multistep planning process for military decisionmaking at lower echelons.

For each of the C2 examples listed in Table 1.2, a member of the project team interviewed an active-duty or retired servicemember with two or more years' experience performing that function. Based on the servicemember's experience and a review of available documentation, the servicemember rated the ten problem characteristics. Servicemembers came from the Army, Air Force, and Navy, and all were officers. Because only a single servicemember completed ratings for each C2 example, it was not possible to assess interrater reliability. The accompanying free responses that SMEs gave to justify the ratings establish their face validity. However, additional research is needed to determine interrater reliability and other psychometric properties of the rating scales.

Chess

To demonstrate the problem taxonomy, we first apply it to the game of chess before turning to C2 examples. The goal of chess is to place the opponent's king under the inescapable threat of capture (checkmate). The game is played on an eight-by-eight grid with six different types of pieces, each of which is allowed to move in different ways. Game play is turn-based.

For chess, six problem characteristics are entirely absent, and four are present to a moderate extent (Table 1.4). The primary challenges arise from the size of the state space (i.e., problem complexity) and the inability to reduce complexity by dividing the board into separate subgames (i.e., reducibility). The difficulty of chess for humans and computer programs alike can be further increased by imposing response deadlines.

Sensor Management

To demonstrate the problem taxonomy and the structured interview protocol for a C2 problem, we then applied them to sensor management as performed by an air battle manager aboard an AWACS. The purpose of sensor management is to detect, track, and identify airborne vehicles that may affect friendly operations. Task inputs include guidance for positive identification, rules of engagement, communication with other tactical and operational C2 nodes, and sensor signals.

Table 1.4
Problem Characteristics in Chess

Problem Characteristic	Rating	Comment
High operational tempo	3	Reponses are limited to 5 minutes in blitz chess, 15 minutes in quick chess, and 30 minutes in action chess. Outside tournament play, slower responses are legal but not socially acceptable.
High rate of environment change	0	The board, pieces, and rules of the game never change.
High problem complexity	2	Chess has approximately 10^{50} reachable board states. However, many are not effectively unique. A limited number of moves is available from any state.
Low reducibility	3	Spatial decomposability is limited—one policy is played across the full board. Temporal decomposability is possible. Minimax, alpha-beta pruning, and Monte Carlo tree search (MCTS) work by enumerating and solving for multiple possible future states and can be parallelized.
Low data availability	0	A virtually limitless number of games can be simulated.
High environmental clutter/noise	0	The game does not involve perceptual noise.
Stochasticity of action outcomes	0	The game does not involve stochastic actions.
Low clarity of goals and utility	0	The objective of the game (avoid being checkmated while checkmating the opponent) is clearly defined.
Incompleteness of information	0	The board is fully visible.
High operational risks and benefits	0	Nothing of material value is at stake.

For sensor management, all but two problem characteristics were present to a moderate or large extent (Table 1.5). The primary challenges arise from the relatively high operational tempo, the nonstationary environment, the presence of naturally occurring and adversary-induced environmental clutter, and the substantial operational risks and benefits. Numerous secondary and tertiary challenges exist as well.

Table 1.5
Problem Characteristics in Sensor Management

Problem Characteristic	Rating	Comment
High operational tempo	3	The latency of the AWACS radar limits the timescale of responses. Additionally, signals must be correlated across multiple returns to identify a track.
High rate of environment change	3	Weather, enemy order of battle, and friendly rules of engagement and special instructions may frequently change.
High problem complexity	2	The multitude of actors creates a large state space. The action set consists of multiple radar modes, azimuths, and orientations, which may be interleaved.
Low reducibility	2	Sensor management is composed of multiple subtasks, including selecting radar modes, interpreting radar returns, and identifying and tracking aircraft. Communication with each tactical and operational C2 node constitutes additional subtasks.
Low data availability	2	Vast amounts of data are recorded during missions. Additionally, sensor performance characteristics can be demonstrated on test ranges. Ability to simulate adversary electronic warfare countermeasures is more limited.
High environmental clutter/noise	3	Weather conditions affect sensor performance. Adversaries employ stealth modes and electronic warfare countermeasures to further complicate positive identification and tracking.
Stochasticity of action outcomes	1	Aircraft limiting factors exist, and sensors occasionally malfunction.
Low clarity of goals and utility	1	Clarity of air picture can be quantified in terms of track quality, which depends on latency, resolution, and registration error.
Incompleteness of information	2	A large amount of information is concealed, although a large number of airborne and multidomain assets can improve the air picture.
High operational risks and benefits	3	Poor task performance will likely result in loss of life and aircraft.

CHAPTER TWO

Analysis of Solution Capabilities

Definitions

In Volume 1, we defined a taxonomy of eight AI system capabilities grouped into four categories. The first grouping, *complexity*, which includes a single solution characteristic, computational efficiency, describes how the amount of time/memory that a system needs scales with the size of the problem. This is roughly analogous to the *Big-O notation* used by computer scientists to denote the processor and memory efficiency of algorithms. For instance, if a problem uses exponentially more clock cycles or memory as the size of the problem instance increases, its computational efficiency may prove unfavorable. But sometimes a solution method that appears dubious on this account may prove attractive in practice: for example, the problem instances for the cases of interest may all be small, rendering the intractability of the technique on large instances irrelevant. This is yet another reason why problem characterization ought to proceed with exploring potential solutions: overly broad problem definitions can result in the premature rejection of solutions that ought to have been considered.

The *performance* grouping includes three solution characteristics that aim to capture how well the potential solution is expected to perform. The first of these, *data efficiency*, is primarily for machine learning (ML) methods, and it describes the number of samples required to train a model for adequate performance. Obviously, the implications of this metric depend on one of the problem characteristics included in the previous taxonomy—*data availability*. If large quantities of data are available, poor performance on this metric may prove tolerable. The other two characteristics in the taxonomy, *soundness* and *optimality*, are related but distinct, particularly in practice. Soundness describes whether a system will ever output a wrong answer: if it is sound, it never will. Optimality describes the extent to which the output of the system is expected to deviate from the best possible answer, as scored by the objective function of interest. Obviously, a fully optimal system will be sound, but a sound system does not need to be optimal. For most difficult real-world problems, globally optimal solutions are either unavailable or demand prohibitive resources. In many cases, however, we can find solutions that are locally optimal.

The third grouping comprises two solution characteristics that describe the *flexibility* of the potential solution in the face of real-world complexities, such as novel situations and malformed inputs. The first of these, *robustness*, is defined as the ability to produce reasonable outputs and/or fail gracefully under unanticipated circumstances. This is distinguished from soundness in that robustness includes the ability to process malformed inputs sensibly, for example, by rejecting them. A system could be sound, because it always outputs a correct answer on a well-formed input, but not robust, because it outputs an incorrect answer (which might look well formed on casual inspection) to a malformed input. The other characteristic, *learning*, captures the system's ability to improve performance through training and/or experience.

The final grouping, *practicality*, includes two characteristics that seek to capture the extent to which the potential solution can address human needs. The first of these, *explainability*, describes the ability of an expert human to understand why the system produces the outputs it does. A system with good explainability can output an account of its reasoning that a human can make sense of, even if that line of reasoning was not necessarily one that a human ever would have employed. This is distinct from the ability to find a high-quality solution: the system may have made the same kind of reasoning mistakes that a human nonexpert might make and may have provided the same kind of explanation of that reasoning as that nonexpert. The *assuredness* characteristic describes the ability of an expert human to determine that the system operates as intended. The intended mode of operation is defined relative to the problem characteristics, particularly operational risks and benefits. In practice, this characteristic will often need to account for legal or regulatory requirements that may not have been designed to account for nonhuman decisionmakers.

Structured Interview Protocols

As we did for C2 problem characteristics, we created a structured protocol to enable valid and reliable scoring of solution capabilities for a given AI system. The goal of the protocol was to determine the extent to which each characteristic was present in the selected system. To facilitate scoring, we created rating scales with values ranging from 0 (*not present*) to 4 (*present to a large extent*). The scales contained definitions and examples corresponding with each of the five levels. Table 2.1 contains the rating scale for one solution capability, computational efficiency.

Table 2.1
Sample Rating Scale for Computational Efficiency

Computational Efficiency
How the amount of time/memory that a system needs scales with the size of the problem

Rating	Definition	Example
0	The computational time/memory needed increases **exponentially** with problem size.	*The planners are testing a tanker planning algorithm. It requires 8 seconds for two tankers, 54 seconds for four tankers, and 2000 seconds for eight tankers.*
1	The computational time/memory needed increases as a **polynomial** of problem size.	*The planners are testing a tanker planning algorithm. It requires 4 seconds for two tankers, 16 seconds for four tankers, and 64 seconds for eight tankers.*
2	The computational time/memory needed increases **linearly** with problem size.	*The planners are testing a tanker planning algorithm. It requires 4 seconds for two tankers, 8 seconds for four tankers, and 16 seconds for eight tankers.*
3	The computational time/memory needed increases **logarithmically** with problem size.	*The planners are testing a tanker planning algorithm. It requires 4 seconds for two tankers, 6 seconds for four tankers, and 8 seconds for eight tankers.*
4	The computational time/memory needed remains **constant** as the problem size increases.	*The planners are testing a tanker planning algorithm. No matter the number of tankers, the algorithm finishes in the same amount of time.*

Application to Specific Artificial Intelligence Systems and Methods

Using the solution taxonomy and the structured interview protocol, we analyzed ten AI systems. The results are summarized in Volume 1. The systems are representative of classic and contemporary approaches in AI. Some of the systems involve learning, and others involve substantial upfront knowledge engineering. Additionally, the systems vary in terms of their suitability for reactive-, planning-, and classification-type tasks. In total, the sample contains an extremely diverse set of AI approaches reflective of those being pursued by the Department of Defense (DoD). The systems are described in Table 2.2.

Next we look in detail at three pairwise combinations of AI systems or methods: Deep Q-Learning versus iterated-width (IW) planning, alpha-beta pruning versus AlphaZero, and a mixed-integer program (MIP) versus a greedy heuristic (GH). These analyses help illustrate how the taxonomy may be used as a tool for comparison.

Comparison of Deep Q-Learning to Iterated-Width Planning

Two AI approaches, Deep Q-Learning and IW planning, have been applied to numerous real-time strategy games and, given their high levels of demonstrated play, have been suggested to be relevant to DoD missions.[1] These approaches have very different origins: Deep Q-Learning arose from work on learning systems and reflects the convergence of deep neural network (DNN) and reinforcement learning (RL). In Deep Q-Learning, a DNN is applied as the subfunction to estimate the value (or "Q") function in a model-free RL framework. Unlike some other forms of RL (such as AlphaZero, described below), model-free RL does not exploit specified or learned models or structured exploration to

---

[1] Volodymyr Mnih, Koray Kavukcuoglu, David Silver, Alex Graves, Ioannis Antonoglou, Daan Wierstra, and Martin Riedmiller, *Playing Atari with Deep Reinforcement Learning*, Ithaca, N.Y.: Cornell University, 2013; Wilmer Bandres, Blai Bonet, and Hector Geffner, "Planning with Pixels in (Almost) Real Time," *Thirty-Second AAAI Conference on Artificial Intelligence*, Palo Alto, Calif: AAAI Press, April 2018; U.S. Air Force Scientific Advisory Board, *Technologies for Enabling Resilient Command and Control MDC2 Overview*, Washington, D.C., 2018; G. Zacharias, *Autonomous Horizons: The Way Forward*, Maxwell Air Force Base, Ala.: Air University Press, Curtis E. LeMay Center for Doctrine Development and Education, 2019.

Table 2.2
Description of Artificial Intelligence Systems

AI System	Description
Deep Q-learning	An algorithm that uses a DNN to learn a subfunction that approximates the values (or "Q") of actions available to an agent in a model-free RL framework.
IW planning	An automated planner that chooses which branches to explore based on their novelty, as embodied in the concept of "width." Branches are only explored if they contain features or combinations of features that have not yet been seen.
AlphaZero	A general RL algorithm for game play that combines two components: a DNN that encodes the approximate values of board states and an MCTS algorithm that simulates games forward from their current state until an end state is reached.
Alpha-beta pruning	An adversarial search algorithm that stops evaluating lines of play that could be exploited by a rational opponent.
MIP	A mathematical optimization program in which some or all variables are restricted to be integers. When solved using branch and bound, only those branches of the potential solution space that could possibly produce a solution better than the best one yet found are explored.
GH	A domain-specific heuristic for MAAP that allocates resources to targets in order of their priority until all resources are exhausted.
Instance-based learning	An approach from cognitive science that retrieves previous experiences stored in memory based on the time since they were encoded and the similarity between the current context and the context in which they were encoded.
Recurrent neural network	A class of neural networks that allow previous outputs to be used as inputs to exhibit temporal dynamic behavior.
Influence network	A probabilistic model of causality that uses Bayesian updates to predict the probabilities of different outcomes given different actions and to select actions.
Genetic algorithm	A search heuristic inspired by natural selection in which a population of candidate solutions are evaluated by a fitness function. The best performing solutions are retained and combined to produce subsequent generations of solutions.

find good-quality moves. Instead, all knowledge is learned from experience and stored in the learned value function.

IW planning arose from research on automated planners. Historically, most automated planners worked by selecting promising branches to explore based on their "distance" from the goal state, as approximated by domain-specific heuristics. IW planning, in contrast, chooses branches based on their novelty, as embodied in the concept of "width."[2] Branches are only explored if they contain features or combinations of features that have never been seen before. Nir Lipovetzky and Hector Geffner empirically demonstrated that IW planning compares favorably to classical planners, despite its simplicity. Moreover, a variant of the approach called rollout-based IW can plan with a simulator as opposed to an explicit model. This means that IW planning can be applied to many of the same tasks as Deep Q-Learning, such as Atari games.[3] Table 2.3 compares the two methods.

Deep Q-Learning and IW planning have very different capabilities:

- *Computational complexity.* For planning tasks, the computational complexity of Deep Q-Learning for finding an optimal solution is polynomial in practice given suitable priors and/or task representations.[4] For reactive tasks, the computational complexity of Deep Q-Learning is far lower given that the learned policy essentially encodes stimulus-response mappings. The complexity of IW planning is dependent on the complexity of the goal rather than the action or state spaces and is the same for deliberate and reactive tasks.[5]
- *Data Efficiency.* One of the major limitations of Deep Q-Learning is its poor sample efficiency: enormous amounts of data and train-

---

[2]   Nir Lipovetzky and Hector Geffner, "Width and Serialization of Classical Planning Problems," *ECAI '12: Proceedings of the 20th European Conference on Artificial Intelligence,* Amsterdam: IOS Press, August 2012.

[3]   Bandres, Bonet, and Geffner, 2018.

[4]   Sven Koenig and Reid G. Simmons, *Complexity Analysis of Real-Time Reinforcement Learning,* Pittsburgh, Pa.: School of Computer Science Carnegie Mellon University, 1993, pp. 99–107.

[5]   Lipovetzky and Geffner, 2012.

Table 2.3
Solution Capabilities of Deep Q-Learning and Iterated-Width Planning

Solution Capability	Deep Q-Learning	IW Planning
Computational efficiency	1/4[a]	1
Data efficiency	0	4
Soundness	1	4
Optimality	3	3
Robustness	0	3
Learning	3	0
Explainability	0	3
Assuredness	0	3

[a] Exponential for planning tasks and logarithmic for reactive tasks.

ing time are often required for good performance. IW planning, by contrast, is not a learning method and does not require training data at all, but it does demand the availability of an accurate simulator or state transition model.

- *Soundness.* Model-free RL methods such as Deep Q-Learning can be unsound: for instance, in some cases they can suggest moves that are not available in a particular state. IW planners, by contrast, are guaranteed to find sound solutions so long as the simulator or state transition model they employ is sound.

- *Optimality.* Neither method offers optimality guarantees, yet both have demonstrated levels of performance commensurate with the most skilled humans.

- *Robustness.* When encountering novel situations, Deep Q-Learning can break or recommend nonsensical actions. IW planning, meanwhile, is as robust as its simulator or state transition model. Moreover, it is sometimes possible to flag situations that break the simulator used by IW planning to allow for countermeasures, such as requesting human advice.

- *Learning.* RL, by definition, is able to learn. Moreover, some forms of RL offer performance guarantees—given enough data and training time, the agent is guaranteed to discover a nearly optimal policy. IW planning does not learn, and therefore its performance does not improve with experience.

- *Explainability.* The policies and state values learned by Deep Q-Learning are typically difficult for humans to interpret. The DNN representing the value function can be queried for its response to particular inputs, but for a nontrivial problem, the input space is too large for comprehensive exploration to be practical. In contrast, the reasoning process used by IW planning to find a solution is comprehensible by humans (even if it is not necessarily one that a human would ever use). Further, the history of state exploration by the IW planner can be used to reconstruct how it recommended a decision.

- *Assuredness.* A major shortcoming of model-free RL methods, such as Deep Q-Learning, is the difficulty of verification and validation (V&V). With IW planners, if the simulator or state transition model is valid, the planner is valid as well.

Comparison of AlphaZero to Alpha-Beta Pruning

As another example of using the solution taxonomy to compare AI systems, the AlphaZero deep reinforcement learning (DRL) system has recently overtaken alpha-beta pruning as the most effective algorithm for playing chess. The respective approaches of AlphaZero and alpha-beta pruning are technically very different. AlphaZero combines two components: a DNN that encodes the approximate values of board states and an MCTS algorithm that simulates games forward from their current state until an end state is reached.[6] The DNN is learned off-line through self-play, and the MCTS is implemented online with self-play. Alpha-beta pruning, in contrast, is a classic search algorithm that prospectively expands potential game states, assuming that for each game state both agents will select optimal moves.[7] The agent then

---

[6]   David Silver, Thomas Hubert, Julian Schrittwieser, Ioannis Antonoglou, Matthew Lai, Arthur Guez, Marc Lanctot, Laurent Sifre, Dharshan Kumaran, Thore Graepel, Timothy Lillicrap, Karen Simonyan, and Demis Hassabi, "A General Reinforcement Learning Algorithm that Masters Chess, Shogi, and Go Through Self-Play," *Science,* Vol. 362, No. 6419, December 2018.

[7]   S. Russell and P. Norvig, *Introduction to Artificial Intelligence: A Modern Approach,* New Delhi: Prentice-Hall of India, 1995.

chooses the move for the current game state that is expected to produce the most attractive future state. Because it is not computationally
feasible to fully expand the game tree, search terminates at a specified
depth, at which point a heuristic is used to estimate the values of different intermediate game states that have been reached.

AlphaZero and alpha-beta pruning also have very different capabilities (Table 2.4). To summarize some key distinctions: AlphaZero

Table 2.4
Solution Capabilities of AlphaZero and Alpha-Beta Pruning

Solution Capability	AlphaZero	Alpha-Beta Pruning	Rationale
Computational efficiency	3	3	Heavy rollouts in AlphaZero require a large amount of simulated online play. The number of branches that alpha-beta pruning explores increases in polynomial time with search depth.
Data efficiency	0	4	AlphaZero approximates game values based on hundreds of centuries of simulated self-play. Alpha-beta pruning does not need training data.
Soundness	4	4	Both approaches can only recommend legal board moves.
Optimality	3	2	Though not provably optimal, AlphaZero outperforms all other known chess players. Though optimal in the limit, alpha-beta pruning is exploitable on the basis of its finite search depth and the heuristics it employs.
Robustness	0	2	Although AlphaZero can be trained for different games, it does not generalize knowledge from one game to another. Alpha-beta pruning is as general as the model and heuristics that it employs.
Learning	3	0	AlphaZero is a learning architecture, although it is infeasible to train it online. Alpha-beta pruning is not capable of learning.
Explainability	0	4	AlphaZero's policy cannot be explained to humans. The alpha-beta search rule is explainable, and the heuristics are often modeled after human decision processes.
Assuredness	0	4	AlphaZero cannot be formally verified. Alpha-beta pruning can be verified by checking the model and heuristics.

is trained using hundreds of centuries of self-play, whereas alpha-beta pruning requires expert knowledge but no training data. AlphaZero is near optimal in that no other human or AI system outperforms it. However, the manner in which AlphaZero achieves such a high level of play complicates V&V and also limits explainability. Alpha-beta pruning is suboptimal, but it can be verified and validated, and its moves can be explained. Finally, AlphaZero can learn lines of play that do not require—or that go beyond—expert knowledge. Yet AlphaZero's data-intensive learning methods limit the possibility of online learning. Alpha-beta pruning is only as capable as the heuristics provided to it by human experts and does not improve further with experience.

Comparison of a Mixed Integer Program and a Greedy Heuristic

Finally, the solution taxonomy can be used to compare AI systems intended for use with C2 process. For example, the MAAP is the time-phased air and space scheme of maneuver for a given ATO period. Among other things, the MAAP assigns aircraft to packages and packages to targets to achieve the effects specified on the joint integrated prioritized target list. The scheduling problem can be specified as a set of constraints and solved using MIP techniques. Alternatively, the scheduling problem can be solved using a simple GH—for example, "schedule missions in order of priority until all resources have been exhausted."[8]

The MIP and the GH have very different capabilities (Table 2.5). Both methods begin from the root of valid solutions and so are guaranteed to provide sound schedules. Neither method uses training data nor improves further with experience. Given sufficient computational resources, the MIP will reduce the optimality gap to an arbitrary degree. Yet, relative to the GH, the MIP's optimality comes at the expense of computational efficiency and explainability.

---

[8] Kevin. J. Rossillon, *Optimized Air Asset Scheduling Within a Joint Aerospace Operations Center*, Cambridge, Mass.: MIT Press, 2015. Additional details about the MIP and the heuristic are provided in Chapter 5.

Table 2.5
Solution Capabilities of Mixed-Integer Program and Greedy Heuristic

Solution Capability	MIP	GH	Rationale
Computational efficiency	0	4	MIP time complexity increases in polynomial time with number of variables. GH increases in linear time or less with number of variables.
Data efficiency	4	4	Neither method uses training data.
Soundness	4	4	Both methods begin from the root of valid solutions.
Optimality	4	1	Given sufficient run time, the MIP will return a solution within the desired optimality gap. No guarantees can be provided about the quality of the GH solution.
Robustness	2	2	Changes to the problem can affect the MIP solve time or the GH's solution quality.
Learning	0	0	Neither method learns.
Explainability	3	4	Although the rationale behind the MIP can be explained, the manner in which it improves solutions is difficult to track and intuit. The GH is based on how a human performs the task.
Assuredness	4	4	The MIP can be verified by checking the potentially large number of constraints. The GH can be formally verified.

CHAPTER THREE

Expert Panel Design, Implementation, and Additional Results

This chapter contains additional details about the design, implementation, and results of the expert panel. The panel followed a structured approach whereby individuals answered questions during two rounds. Between rounds, they reviewed summaries of one another's responses. This approach, called a Delphi panel, can be used to collect and share informed judgments and to build consensus among experts. As of yet, the literature does not contain an agreed on mapping from problem characteristics to required solution capabilities. The purpose of conducting a Delphi panel was to build such a mapping from the informed judgments of AI experts.

Panel Design and Implementation

The panel was conducted using ExpertLens—an online, modified-Delphi platform. Each round of the panel took place over about ten days. Round 1 was open from November 18 to November 27, Round 2 was open from December 3 to December 12, and Round 3 was open from December 13 to December 23.

In Rounds 1 and 3, experts were asked to rate the importance of solution capabilities for the different problem characteristics. The rounds contained ten study pages. One problem characteristic was presented at the top of each page. The eight solution capabilities were displayed below the problem characteristic (Figure 3.1). Experts selected

Figure 3.1
Sample Round 1 and Round 3 Response Section Interfaces

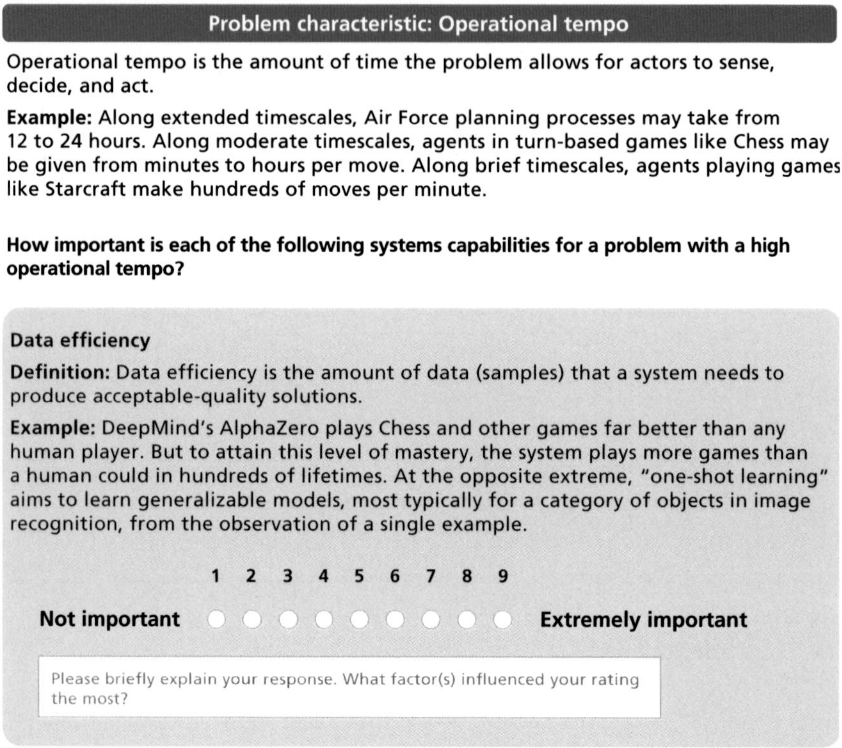

> ### Problem characteristic: Operational tempo
>
> Operational tempo is the amount of time the problem allows for actors to sense, decide, and act.
>
> **Example:** Along extended timescales, Air Force planning processes may take from 12 to 24 hours. Along moderate timescales, agents in turn-based games like Chess may be given from minutes to hours per move. Along brief timescales, agents playing games like Starcraft make hundreds of moves per minute.
>
> **How important is each of the following systems capabilities for a problem with a high operational tempo?**
>
> ---
>
> **Data efficiency**
>
> **Definition:** Data efficiency is the amount of data (samples) that a system needs to produce acceptable-quality solutions.
>
> **Example:** DeepMind's AlphaZero plays Chess and other games far better than any human player. But to attain this level of mastery, the system plays more games than a human could in hundreds of lifetimes. At the opposite extreme, "one-shot learning" aims to learn generalizable models, most typically for a category of objects in image recognition, from the observation of a single example.
>
>   1 2 3 4 5 6 7 8 9
>
> **Not important** ○ ○ ○ ○ ○ ○ ○ ○ ○ **Extremely important**
>
> > Please briefly explain your response. What factor(s) influenced your rating the most?

a radio button to rate the importance of each solution capability for the problem characteristic, and they provided explanations in a text box below the rating scale. The order of problem characteristics across pages and the sequence of solution capabilities within pages were randomized across experts.

In Round 2, experts viewed a bar chart with the distribution of ratings for each problem-solution pair (Figure 3.2). The bar chart marked the expert's Round 1 response with a red point and the median response with a vertical blue line. A table appeared beside the bar chart. The table contained thematic groupings of responses given by experts for ratings of low, moderate, and high importance.

Figure 3.2
Sample Round 2 Response Summary

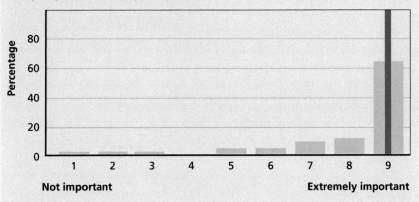

> ### Problem characteristic: Operational tempo
>
> **Data efficiency**
>
> **Definition:** Data efficiency is the amount of data (samples) that a system needs to produce acceptable-quality solutions.
>
> **Example:** DeepMind's AlphaZero plays Chess and other games far better than any human player. But to attain this level of mastery, the system plays more games than a human could in hundreds of lifetimes. At the opposite extreme, "one-shot learning" aims to learn generalizable models, most typically for a category of objects in image recognition, from the observation of a single example.
>
> **Group responses from 44 participants**
>
> *Percentage* (y-axis: 0, 20, 40, 60, 80)
> (x-axis: 1 2 3 4 5 6 7 8 9)
> **Not important** .... **Extremely important**
>
> | Reasons For | Comment Summary |
> | --- | --- |
> | Low ratings (1–3) | |
> | Uncertain ratings (4–6) | |
> | High ratings (7–9) | • Data efficiency is the direct approach for dealing with low data availability |
>
> View Participants' Round One Comments
>
> **Round Two discussion**
>
> New discussion topic

Data Analysis

Because of the bounded nature of the response scale, we used median values to measure central tendencies. To determine whether participants agreed for each problem-solution pair, we followed the method described by D. Khodyakov and his colleagues.[1] We first calculated the interpercentile range:

Interpercentile Range = 70th percentile − 30th percentile.

We then calculated the interpercentile range adjusted for symmetry:

Interpercentile Range Adjusted for Asymmetry =
2.35 + (Asymmetry Index × 1.5).

The asymmetry index equals the magnitude of the difference between the median importance rating and the center of the response scale. When the interpercentile range of responses exceeds the interpercentile range adjusted for asymmetry, it indicates that the distribution of ratings is bimodal and that disagreement exists. In the case of no disagreement, we looked to the value of the median response to determine whether the group rated the pair as "Not Important" (lower tertile), "Moderately Important" (middle tertile), or "Extremely Important" (upper tertile).

To better explain importance ratings, we thematically analyzed free responses. As in previous ExpertLens panels, we grouped rationale comments for each problem-solution pair based on the tertiles of the corresponding numerical responses. Two researchers, trained by the principal investigator, reviewed and coded all qualitative comments to identify emergent themes. All coding results were reviewed by the principal investigator, and coding disagreements were discussed and resolved.

---

[1]   D. Khodyakov, S. Grant, B. Denger, K. Kinnett, A. Martin, M. Booth, C. Armstrong, E. Dao, C. Chen, I. Coulter, H. Peay, G. Hazlewood, and N. Street, "Using an Online, Modified Delphi Approach to Engage Patients and Caregivers in Determining the Patient-Centeredness of Duchenne Muscular Dystrophy Care Considerations," *Medical Decision Making*, Vol. 39, No. 8, 2019.

Limitations

The selection of participants was nonrandom, as is typical for expert panels. In addition to being experts in AI, most participants worked in military settings. As such, although the problem characteristics and solution capabilities are general in nature, the results of the expert panel are most applicable to the case of AI in military contexts.

Results

Out of 60 invited individuals, 49 (82 percent) participated in at least one panel round. Out of these 49 individuals, all participated in the first round, 38 participated in the second round (78 percent), and 25 participated in the third round (51 percent). Aggregating across the first and third rounds, experts provided a total of 5,270 numerical ratings and 2,009 written responses.

Expert Ratings

After the first round, the group rated 36 of the 80 problem-solution pairs as "extremely important" (i.e., median rating > 6.5). Disagreement existed for 8 of the 80 pairs. After the third round, group ratings scarcely changed, but disagreement remained for only 3 of the 80 pairs, reflecting increased consensus.

Figure 3.3 shows the median values and ranges of values for each of the 80 problem-solution pairs after Round 3. Stars denote problem-solution pairs where disagreement existed. Vertical lines denote cutoffs between the three categories of responses: "Not Important," "Moderately Important," and "Extremely Important."

To identify potentially redundant problem characteristics, we considered the importance of the eight solution capabilities to each. The correlation was strongest between stochastic action effects and environmental clutter ($r^2 = 0.89$), meaning those problem characteristics called for similar solution capabilities. This is sensible given that both involve dealing with uncertainty. Overall, problem characteristics were only modestly correlated with one another (mean $r^2 = 0.32$), indicating their distinctiveness.

Likewise, to detect potentially redundant solution capabilities, we considered the importance of each to the ten problem characteristics. The

Figure 3.3
Distributions of Ratings by Problem-Solution Pair at Conclusion of Round 3

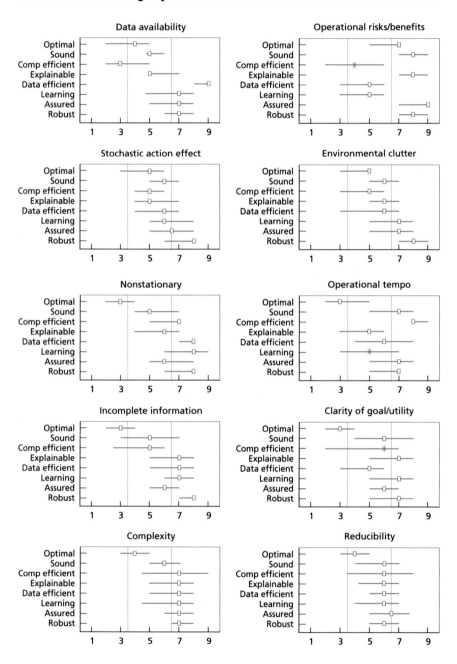

correlation was strongest between soundness and assured ($r^2 = 0.69$), meaning those solution capabilities were called for by similar problem characteristics. This is sensible given that both involve ensuring safe and reasonable performance. Overall, solution capabilities were only modestly correlated with one another (mean $r^2 = 0.22$), indicating their distinctiveness.

Expert Free Responses

To illustrate the types of free responses given by experts, Table 3.1 contains individual expert's responses from nine problem-solution pairs in Round 1. The first three pairs were rated "Extremely Important" by the group. The explanations given are intuitive; consequential problems require assured solutions; data efficiency is needed to deal with low data availability; and robustness is essential for handling noisy environment inputs.

The next three pairs were rated as "Not Important" by the group. Interestingly, all involve one solution capability: optimality. The explanations given address the impossibility of finding optimal solutions and the importance of satisfying other performance criteria, such as speed of response.

The final three pairs were rated as "Moderately Important" by the group but contained a wide range of individual expert responses. In these cases, explanations convey meaningful differences in how experts perceived and rated the importance of a given solution capability for a problem characteristic. For example, some experts considered learning to be extremely important for complex problems because of the infeasibility of hand-coding solutions for such problems. Others considered it too hard to train an agent to perform complex tasks. Some experts considered explainability to be extremely important when operational tempo was high to allow humans to comprehend and accept AI solutions. Others saw explainability as less important due to the limited time humans have to consider how the AI system had arrived at its solution. Finally, some experts considered explainability to be extremely important for irreducible problems to allow humans to accept answers without needing to check all subproblems. Others considered it less important due to the inherent difficulty of explaining and understanding solutions to irreducible problems.

Table 3.1
Experts' Rationale for Ratings in Round 1

Problem Characteristic	Solution Capability	Importance	Quotation
High risks/ benefits	Assured	Extremely	"By definition, it's very important to get the right answer in high-stakes situations."
Low data availability	Data efficient	Extremely	"Given low data availability, the algorithm needs high data efficiency."
Environmental clutter	Robust	Extremely	"Robustness is all-important for dealing with noisy environments."
Low goal/ utility clarity	Optimal	Not	"If goals aren't well defined, optimality is an essentially meaningless concept."
Incomplete information	Optimal	Not	"It is impossible to say something is optimal given many unknowns."
High tempo	Optimal	Not	"If speed is crucial, then you don't have time to find the exactly optimal solution."
Problem complexity	Learning	Not	"Learning likely to be harder in larger problems."
		Extremely	"Difficult to hard code a solution to a complex problem."
Operational tempo	Explainability	Not	"Useful in hindsight, but not usually feasible when a decision needs to be made quickly."
		Extremely	"Need to be able to be quickly summarize for the decisionmaker to trust the system."
Reducibility	Explainability	Not	"If we can't understand irreducible systems, we can't expect AI to explain it to us simply."
		Extremely	"Useful for irreducible problems since it will be harder to check substeps of the solution along the way."

The following set of tables (Tables 3.2–3.11) contain groups of themes reported for all problem-solution pairs. The number of experts giving the response is contained in the parentheses along with the importance rating assigned ("Not Important," "Moderately Important," "Extremely Important"). These give insights into the reasons behind the pairings that the expert panel created.

Table 3.2
Pairing Solution Capabilities to Problem Complexity in Round 1

Solution Capability	Thematic Response
Computational efficiency	• Factors besides algorithm complexity may mitigate run-time constraints. (n = 4, Moderately Important) • Complex problems have huge input sizes, so you must be able to process them efficiently. (n = 13, Extremely Important)
Data efficiency	• The more complex the problem, the more data needed to learn about it, rendering data efficiency. (n = 7, Moderately Important) • If the state space is huge, it is inherently difficult to gather exhaustive training data. This necessitates making the most of the limited training data on hand. (n = 7, Extremely Important) • Data efficiency is important to reduce training time for complex problems. (n = 4, Extremely Important)
Soundness	• Soundness is compromised for complex problems because it depends on how accurately the system developer captures the constraints of the task/environment. (n = 5, Moderately Important) • Soundness is needed to ensure that results are valid across the large input and output spaces. (n = 6, Extremely Important) • As complexity increases, it becomes harder for humans to check solutions and determine their soundness. (n = 2, Extremely Important)
Optimality	• Optimality is likely unobtainable for complex real-world problems. (n = 22, Not Important)
Robustness	• Complex problems may present unanticipated circumstances, warranting robustness. (n = 12, Extremely Important)
Learning	• Learning is likely to be harder for large problems. (n = 3, Moderately Important) • Hard to audit the performance of a learning system on a complex task. (n = 2, Moderately Important) • Too difficult to hard code a solution to a complex problem. (n = 6, Extremely Important)
Explainability	• Results of complex problems may be too hard to explain to a human. (n = 3, Moderately Important) • Humans have greater difficulty understanding complex problems, which calls for greater explainability. (n = 12, Extremely Important)
Assuredness	• Assumes that expert familiar with the problem space can identify what appropriate behavior is, which may be compromised for complex problems. (n = 4, Moderately Important) • More important for highly complex problems because such problems allow for a wide range of outcomes and points of failure. (n = 9, Extremely Important)

NOTE: Values in parentheses show number of observations per thematic response and corresponding importance rating.

Table 3.3
Pairing Solution Capabilities to Reducibility in Round 1

Solution Capability	Thematic Response
Computational efficiency	• Solutions to irreducible problems cannot be parallelized, and so the algorithmic efficiency is important. ($n = 16$, Extremely Important)
Data efficiency	• Models for complex problems require large amounts of data anyways, and so data efficiency does not matter. ($n = 3$, Not Important)
	• The size of irreducible problems argues for data efficient models, since the effective size of training data—relative to problem size—may be quite small. ($n = 8$, Extremely Important)
Soundness	• Since it may be more difficult to find optimal solutions to complex problems, soundness may suffice. ($n = 7$, Extremely Important)
Optimality	• If the goal is to respond faster than the adversary, speed is more important than optimality. ($n = 2$, Not Important)
	• High complexity makes optimality unobtainable in most cases. ($n = 10$, Moderately Important)
Robustness	• Significantly more difficult to maintain stable behavior when problem factors are tightly coupled. ($n = 8$, Extremely Important)
	• Solutions must be robust to error and model misspecification, which may be more likely for complex problems. ($n = 1$, Extremely Important)
	• A complex problem is likely to cause unusual ($n =$ bad) solutions. ($n = 2$, Extremely Important)
Learning	• Learning against an irreducible problem is infeasible/inefficient. ($n = 2$, Not Important)
	• The difficulty of representing a problem and knowledge motivates learning methods. ($n = 9$, Extremely Important)
Explainability	• If we cannot understand irreducible systems, how can we expect AI to explain them to us simply. ($n = 4$, Moderately Important)
	• Useful for irreducible problems because it is not possible to check substeps of the solution along the way. ($n = 8$, Extremely Important)
	• Since irreducible problems' solutions are more opaque, users need more information to trust results. ($n = 2$, Extremely Important)
Assuredness	• Challenging and possibly infeasible for irreducible problems. ($n = 2$, Moderately Important)
	• Necessary to ensure model is functioning properly, especially since output may be more sensitive to inputs in an irreducible system. ($n = 8$, Extremely Important)
	• Since irreducible problems' solutions are more opaque, more information is needed to verify and validate the solution. ($n = 3$, Extremely Important)

NOTE: Values in parentheses show number of observations per thematic response and corresponding importance rating.

Table 3.4
Pairing Solution Capabilities to Rate of Environment Change in Round 1

Solution Capability	Thematic Response
Computational efficiency	• Dynamic environments may drive frequent need to recalculate and to adapt. (n = 8, Extremely Important) • Models may need to relearn parameters relatively quickly. (n = 6, Extremely Important) • You may need real-time dynamic planning capabilities. Speed and low complexity are important for such systems. (n = 3, Extremely Important)
Data efficiency	• Data efficiency governs how quickly a system can adapt to a changing task/environment. (n = 18, Extremely Important) • Data efficiency is important because older data will be less relevant, effectively reducing the training sample. (n = 7, Extremely Important)
Soundness	• With the conditions changing, soundness is less important as any new solution could be rendered obsolete at any moment. (n = 2, Not Important) • Must be able to show that solutions remain valid even as environment changes. (n = 12, Extremely Important)
Optimality	• Hard to effectively compute optimal solutions in nonstationary environments since they change over time. (n = 15, Not Important) • If the goal is to respond faster than the adversary, speed is more important than optimality. (n = 5, Not Important)
Robustness	• Adaptation to change is a key factor driving need for robustness. (n = 15, Extremely Important)
Learning	• Learning may be a liability in a nonstationary environment, due to overweighting stale data. (n = 3, Not Important) • Knowledge transfer, concept discovery, and analogous reasoning may be more important than online learning in a rapidly evolving environment. (n = 4, Moderately Important) • Learning enables adaptation to changing environment. (n = 19, Extremely Important)
Explainability	• Explaining behavior is not as relevant when explanations can quickly become irrelevant. (n = 7, Not Important) • Must know how the system is thinking under dynamic conditions to judge if it is "behind the power curve." (n = 11, Extremely Important) • Explainability is even more important to engender trust in a dynamic environment. (n = 2, Extremely Important)
Assuredness	• More difficult to verify and validate when environment is nonstationary. (n = 4, Moderately Important) • Important to recertify a model or algorithm for a changed environment and to determine when it should be discarded. (n = 5, Extremely Important) • Important that the users understand how well the system responds to changes and what happens while the system is adapting. (n = 2, Extremely Important)

NOTE: Values in parentheses show number of observations per thematic response and corresponding importance rating.

Table 3.5
Pairing Solution Capabilities to Operational Tempo in Round 1

Solution Capability	Thematic Response
Computational efficiency	• With high operational tempo, the algorithm must solve problems quickly. ($n = 24$, Extremely Important)
Data efficiency	• Training is almost always done off-line, in which case data efficiency does not relate to operational tempo. ($n = 14$, Moderately Important) • Data efficiency, in terms of amount of data needed to reach a solution, may be important if there is limited time to gather data. ($n = 5$, Extremely Important)
Soundness	• Assuring soundness may take more compute and decision time. ($n = 1$, Not Important) • Approximation is more important to deliver incremental solutions quickly. ($n = 4$, Moderately Important) • Soundness is critical since speed minimizes a human's ability to verify the AI's solution. ($n = 8$, Extremely Important)
Optimality	• If speed is critical, there may not be time to find optimal solutions. ($n = 20$, Not Important)
Robustness	• High operational tempo may imply a narrowly defined task, making robustness less important. ($n = 4$, Moderately Important) • In a high-tempo setting, there may not be time for a human to double-check the AI output. ($n = 8$, Extremely Important) • In a high-tempo setting, there may not be time to fix a brittle system and to debug. ($n = 2$, Extremely Important)
Learning	• Likely not time for learning with high operational tempo. ($n = 8$, Not Important) • Learning-based algorithms, once trained, are typically much quicker for inference and prediction. ($n = 3$, Extremely Important)
Explainability	• Useful but possibly infeasible when a decision needs to be made quickly. ($n = 13$, Not Important) • Explanation might be costly algorithmically. ($n = 2$, Moderately Important) • Explainability engenders trust, which is important if it reduces time the human spends checking the AI. ($n = 3$, Extremely Important)
Assuredness	• V&V desirable because there is less time for a human to check outputs. ($n = 9$, Extremely Important)

NOTE: Values in parentheses show number of observations per thematic response and corresponding importance rating.

Table 3.6
Pairing Solution Capabilities to Data Availability in Round 1

Solution Capability	Thematic Response
Computational efficiency	• If training data is the limiting factor, a sophisticated algorithm may be needed to overcome that. (n = 8, Not Important) • Greater algorithm complexity is tolerable since it only has a small amount of data to run on. (n = 4, Not Important)
Data efficiency	• Data efficiency is the direct approach for dealing with low data availability. (n = 25, Extremely Important)
Soundness	• Ensuring soundness may be impossible with low data availability. (n = 4, Not Important) • Important to have soundness when working with sparse data to avoid overfitting. (n = 4, Moderately Important) • Because the variable space is undersampled, soundness is more important. (n = 2, Extremely Important)
Optimality	• Without sufficient training data, it is inherently difficult to optimize the objective function. (n = 12, Not Important)
Robustness	• It is not feasible to produce robust models when there is little data for training. (n = 4, Moderately Important) • Robustness is necessary with limited data, as there are likely gaps in coverage of possible inputs. (n = 11, Extremely Important)
Learning	• In general, learning is hampered by low data, motivating the use of alternate model-based methods. (n = 3, Not Important) • Given little prior data, it is important to continue adapting and learning online. (n = 12, Extremely Important)
Explainability	• Complexity of mathematical solutions to small data problems will make them hard to explain. (n = 1, Not Important) • Given less data, it may be easier to explain a decision. (n = 2, Moderately Important) • If there is not much data to use, you must be sure that the system is appropriately using the data it does have. (n = 9, Extremely Important)
Assuredness	• Difficult to verify and validate if little data is available for testing. (n = 2, Moderately Important) • V&V needed to characterize and bound error, determining when an algorithm does not have enough data to be effective. (n = 4, Extremely Important)

NOTE: Values in parentheses show number of observations per thematic response and corresponding importance rating.

Table 3.7
Pairing Solution Capabilities to Environmental Clutter in Round 1

Capability	Thematic Response
Computational efficiency	• More computational resources must be dedicated to preprocessing noisy data. ($n = 9$, Moderately Important) • If computation requirements are more taxed in a noisy environment, low algorithmic complexity may be desirable. ($n = 4$, Moderately Important) • With more noise, iteration will be important—an algorithm should propose a solution and allow humans to interact with the solution. ($n = 1$, Extremely Important)
Data efficiency	• Data efficiency can be a liability in a noisy data set—an algorithm that converges quickly on a good solution in a clean data set can converge quickly on a bad solution in a noisy one. ($n = 3$, Not Important) • Data containing systematic/environment noise will typically require more data collection to overcome noise. ($n = 14$, Moderately Important) • Data efficiency can, in a supervised setting, enable the development of practical noise filters. ($n = 2$, Extremely Important)
Soundness	• In a noisy environment, formal soundness is too strict of a standard. ($n = 6$, Not Important) • Rectifying noise and providing a sound solution is critical in a noisy environment. ($n = 7$, Extremely Important)
Optimality	• With lots of noise, optimality is not possible. ($n = 12$, Not Important) • A system may be designed to optimally cope with clutter/noise. ($n = 2$, Moderately Important)
Robustness	• Robustness is all-important for dealing with noisy environments. ($n = 19$, Extremely Important)
Learning	• Learning in cluttered environment may be risky due to overfitting and/or inefficiency. ($n = 5$, Not Important) • Both learning and nonlearning systems can be designed to handle noise. ($n = 2$, Moderately Important) • The ability to learn statistical regularities seems especially useful in a noisy environment. ($n = 14$, Extremely Important) • It may be impossible to anticipate noise encountered in an operational environment, making online learning critical. ($n = 2$, Extremely Important)
Explainability	• Explainability is even harder in case of noisy inputs and may not be worth the effort. ($n = 8$, Not Important) • With noisy inputs, it is important to know why the algorithm makes a particular choice. ($n = 11$, Extremely Important)
Assuredness	• Infeasible in noisy environments—the system may work as intended but produce bad results because of noisy inputs. ($n = 3$, Moderately Important) • Effective V&V can ensure an approach is suitable given different models of noise. ($n = 15$, Extremely Important)

NOTE: Values in parentheses show number of observations per thematic response and corresponding importance rating.

Table 3.8
Pairing Solution Capabilities to Clarity of Utility/Goals in Round 1

Capability	Thematic Response
Computational efficiency	• If goals are unclear, the algorithm must explore multiple possible solutions, which is enabled by low complexity. ($n = 13$, Extremely Important)
Data efficiency	• Data efficiency can be a liability in a noisy data set—an algorithm that converges quickly on a good solution in a clean data set can converge quickly on a bad solution in a noisy one. ($n = 3$, Not Important) • Data containing systematic/environment noise will typically require more data collection to overcome noise. ($n = 14$, Moderately Important) • Data efficiency can, in a supervised setting, enable the development of practical noise filters. ($n = 2$, Extremely Important)
Soundness	• Without clarity about the goals/utility of end states, it may not be possible to evaluate soundness. ($n = 2$, Not Important) • Since optimal solutions are not definable, soundness is relatively more important. ($n = 14$, Extremely Important)
Optimality	• If goals are not well defined, optimality is a meaningless concept. ($n = 19$, Not Important)
Robustness	• The model should perform robustly across a range of possible goals. ($n = 10$, Extremely Important)
Learning	• Many types of learning are critically dependent on clearly stated goals and objectives. ($n = 8$, Moderately Important) • Algorithms can learn even weakly favored preference. ($n = 12$, Extremely Important) • Learning may be important to adapt to changing preferences. ($n = 3$, Extremely Important)
Explainability	• Explanations of AI outputs may help humans gain clarity on goals and utility. ($n = 10$, Extremely Important) • When goals/utility functions are ill defined, it is more important to understand how the system works since it is not optimizing against a known criterion. ($n = 10$, Extremely Important)
Assuredness	• V&V is ill defined if the intended purpose of the system is not clear. ($n = 10$, Moderately Important) • Because objective performance measures are lacking, V&V is needed to give confidence in the system. ($n = 3$, Extremely Important)

NOTE: Values in parentheses show number of observations per thematic response and corresponding importance rating.

Table 3.9
Pairing Solution Capabilities to Stochasticity of Action Outcomes in Round 1

Capability	Thematic Response
Computational efficiency	• If outcomes appear stochastic because of the complexity of the problem, a complex model may be needed to account for that. ($n = 4$, Not Important) • Problems with stochastic action outcomes require more training/sampling, so lower complexity is important. ($n = 11$, Moderately Important)
Data efficiency	• Data efficiency is less important because, given stochastic outcomes, more data are needed anyway to make accurate predictions. ($n = 17$, Moderately Important) • Incorporating model-based methods of effector outcomes can provide significant gains without requiring additional samples. ($n = 2$, Moderately Important)
Soundness	• Not feasible with stochastic outputs. ($n = 5$, Moderately Important) • The inherent uncertainty of stochastic problems makes it important to ensure that solutions are sound. ($n = 9$, Extremely Important)
Optimality	• The stochastic nature of action outcomes means that optimality is effectively impossible. ($n = 13$, Not Important) • A system may be designed to optimally cope with stochastic action outputs. ($n = 5$, Extremely Important)
Robustness	• Stochastic actions entail unexpected outcomes, which call for robustness. ($n = 15$, Extremely Important)
Learning	• Stochasticity and learning might be diametrically opposed due to the risk of learning false patterns and the inefficiency of learning. ($n = 5$, Moderately Important) • Building probabilistic action models may require sampling and learning. ($n = 6$, Extremely Important) • Because stochastic outcomes can produce states not experienced in the training set, the system will need to continue to learn online. ($n = 5$, Extremely Important)
Explainability	• Explainability is inherently difficult in a stochastic system. ($n = 4$, Not Important) • Explanation may help to make sense of unexpected outputs and to properly attribute failure to the stochastic environment. ($n = 10$, Extremely Important)
Assuredness	• V&V in a stochastic system is difficult and may require unrealistic amounts of test data. ($n = 4$, Not Important) • Given inevitable errors due to stochastic nature of action outcomes, V&V is needed to ensure that failures are not attributable to the system. ($n = 6$, Extremely Important)

NOTE: Values in parentheses show number of observations per thematic response and corresponding importance rating.

Table 3.10
Pairing Solution Capabilities to Incomplete Information in Round 1

Capability	Thematic Response
Computational efficiency	• A complex algorithm may be needed to resolve imperfect information. ($n = 5$, Not Important) • With incomplete information, an algorithm may need to explore enormous numbers of combinations of plausible data sets, making efficiency important. ($n = 8$, Extremely Important)
Data efficiency	• If compensating for incomplete information with learning, data efficiency becomes important. ($n = 5$, Moderately Important) • Data demands are larger with incomplete information, so we need a more efficient learner. ($n = 9$, Extremely Important)
Soundness	• Concept of soundness is less important if we have limited faith in our assumptions about the problem to begin with. ($n = 8$, Not Important) • Soundness is essential despite gaps in knowledge. ($n = 4$, Extremely Important)
Optimality	• Impossible to say something is optimal given many unknowns. ($n = 19$, Not Important)
Robustness	• Robustness is central to dealing with unknowns in problems of uncertain information. ($n = 18$, Extremely Important)
Learning	• Learning is important for systems to improve at generalizing over incomplete information. ($n = 13$, Extremely Important) • Online learning is particularly important in cases where additional information is gained during task performance. ($n = 9$, Extremely Important)
Explainability	• Relatively less important since the model is building in lots of assumptions anyway. ($n = 5$, Moderately Important)
Assuredness	• V&V is only possible to the extent that information about the problem is available. ($n = 2$, Not Important) • Particularly important given that the AI's performance may be questionable when given incomplete information. ($n = 6$, Extremely Important)

NOTE: Values in parentheses show number of observations per thematic response and corresponding importance rating.

Table 3.11
Pairing Solution Capabilities to Operational Risks and Benefits in Round 1

Capability	Thematic Response
Computational efficiency	• Whether algorithm works, irrespective of complexity, is all that matters. ($n = 8$, Not Important) • If operational risks are time sensitive, low complexity becomes essential. ($n = 6$, Extremely Important) • High-risk situations are more likely to involve humans. Models are only useful if they can integrate with human planners frequently. ($n = 2$, Extremely Important)
Data efficiency	• Given high stakes, extra data may be collected if needed to produce quality outputs. ($n = 5$, Not Important)
Soundness	• Given the criticality of the application, the output must be sound. ($n = 16$, Extremely Important)
Optimality	• Optimality is unobtainable for most real-world problems. ($n = 3$, Not Important) • Good/useful outputs need not be optimal. ($n = 6$, Moderately Important) • In a high-stakes situation, optimizing performance is important. ($n = 8$, Extremely Important)
Robustness	• High-risk situations are more likely to involve humans, reducing the need for robust algorithmic solutions. ($n = 1$, Moderately Important) • Robustness is important to ensure that a system does not break down during critical tasks. ($n = 1$, Moderately Important) • Catastrophic failure is unacceptable when critical decisions must be made. ($n = 15$, Extremely Important)
Learning	• A preprogrammed system may be preferred if the risks associated with it are better understood. ($n = 2$, Not Important) • Due to their trial-and-error nature, learning systems may commit mistakes that must be avoided in highly consequential settings. ($n = 6$, Moderately Important)
Explainability	• Given the need for human support for highly consequential decisions, explainability provides trust and insight into the solution process. ($n = 16$, Extremely Important) • It may be unethical to make life-affecting decisions based on unexplained algorithms. ($n = 2$, Extremely Important)
Assuredness	• High risk/reward scenarios require assured components. ($n = 9$, Extremely Important) • V&V needed to ensure that users understand model strengths, weaknesses, and credible uses. ($n = 2$, Extremely Important)

NOTE: Values in parentheses show number of observations per thematic response and corresponding importance rating.

CHAPTER FOUR

Metrics for Evaluating Artificial Intelligence Solutions

This chapter provides additional detail on the development of the three categories of metrics. There is additional analysis and, finally, a notional "scorecard" for operationalizing these measures.

Review of Strategic Guidance

In 2012, DoD published DoD Directive 3000.09, *Autonomy in Weapon Systems*. This document described the challenges associated with V&V and test and evaluation (T&E) of autonomous systems. The directive required that "plans [be] in place for V&V and T&E to establish system reliability, effectiveness, and suitability under realistic conditions, including possible adversary actions." While not explicitly written for AI solutions, these requirements clearly apply to AI in many cases, especially for autonomous systems that are run by AI. The Joint Artificial Intelligence Center expects to update this directive, along with other policy recommendations, in 2020.[1]

In response to the growing interest in AI and ML over the past few years, many other national- and DoD-level strategy documents have recognized the complexity of the assessment process for AI algorithms and, accordingly, have highlighted the need for better metrics and testing environments. While this list is not meant to be exhaustive,

---

[1] Justin Doubleday, "Pentagon Reviewing Policy on Autonomy in Weapon Systems amid Advances in Artificial Intelligence," *Inside Defense*, February 28, 2020.

the set of major reports and directives certainly includes the following (in alphabetical order):

- Defense Innovation Board, *AI Principles: Recommendations on the Ethical Use of Artificial Intelligence by the Department of Defense*, 2019
- Defense Science Board, *Summer Study on Autonomy*, 2016
- DoD, *Artificial Intelligence Strategy*, 2018
- National Science and Technology Council (NSTC) Committee on AI, *The National Artificial Intelligence Research and Development Strategic Plan: 2019 Update*, White House Office of Science and Technology Policy (OSTP), 2019
- NSTC Committee on Science and Technology Enterprise, *Federal Cybersecurity Research and Development Strategic Plan*, White House OSTP, 2019
- NSTC Committee on Technology, *Preparing for the Future of Artificial Intelligence*, White House OSTP, 2016
- National Security Commission on Artificial Intelligence, *Interim Report*, 2019
- National Institute of Standards and Technology, *U.S. Leadership in AI: A Plan for Federal Engagement in Developing Technical Standards and Related Tools*, 2019
- President Trump, *Executive Order on Maintaining American Leadership in Artificial Intelligence*, 2019.

In addition to the strategic guidance on AI solutions, we also reviewed several documents on C2 problems and C2 assessment. These documents include the following (in alphabetical order):

- Air Force Doctrine, Annex 3-30, *Command and Control*, 2020a
- Army Doctrine Publication 6-0, Mission Command, *Command and Control of Army Forces*, 2019
- Joint Publication 3-0, *Joint Operations*, 2017
- Marine Corps Doctrinal Publication 6, *Command and Control*, 2018
- North Atlantic Treaty Organization Research and Technology Organization, *Code of Best Practice for C2 Assessment*, 2002.

Several common themes emerged from our review of these documents. The first concerns the importance of T&E/V&V for AI in general. We find broad agreement that T&E is complicated and that new methods are needed to assess software that can learn and adapt. As the Defense Innovation Board explains,[2]

> For legacy systems, robust Test and Evaluation (T&E) and Verification and Validation (V&V) processes are well established, both mathematically as well as institutionally. However, for newer forms of ML, for example, T&E and V&V face serious challenges because there are open research questions within the field of AI about how best to achieve these. Additionally, for ML systems that learn over their lifetime, challenges remain for continual certification that these systems do not learn behaviors outside of their intended use and parameters. For multiple agent systems, as well as for interacting AI systems, the ability to model complexity and emergent behaviors is not well understood.

We also find four key implementation issues: explainability/credibility, human-machine teaming, safety and security, and reliability.[3] While not unique to AI solutions, these issues are particularly important for them. For example, a strategic priority of NSTC's strategic plan is to "ensure the safety and security of AI systems [and] advance knowledge of how to design AI systems that are reliable, dependable, safe, and trustworthy."[4] In Table 4.1, we summarize which of these issues are mentioned in which document.

In addition to the strategic guidance on AI solutions, we also reviewed several documents on C2 problems and C2 assessment in general from the Army, Marines, North Atlantic Treaty Organization, and joint doctrine. We discuss these in more detail when we discuss effectiveness.

---

[2] Defense Innovation Board, *AI Principles: Recommendations on the Ethical Use of Artificial Intelligence by the Department of Defense*, Arlington, Va., 2019.

[3] We define these terms later in this section when we define their associated metrics categories.

[4] Select Committee on Artificial Intelligence, *The National Artificial Intelligence Research and Development Strategic Plan: 2019 Update*, Washington, D.C.: National Science and Technology Council, June 2019.

Table 4.1
Implementation Issues Highlighted in Strategic Guidance Documents

Document	Explainability/ Credibility	Safety and Security	Human-Machine Teaming	Reliability
Defense Innovation Board, *AI Principles: Recommendations on the Ethical Use of Artificial Intelligence by the Department of Defense*, 2019	✓	✓		✓
Defense Science Board, *Summer Study on Autonomy*, 2016	✓	✓	✓	
DoD, *Artificial Intelligence Strategy*, 2018	✓	✓	✓	✓
NSTC Committee on Artificial Intelligence, *The National Artificial Intelligence Research and Development Strategic Plan*: 2019 Update, 2019	✓	✓	✓	✓
NSTC Committee on Science and Technology Enterprise, *Federal Cybersecurity Research and Development Strategic Plan*, 2019	✓	✓		
NSTC Committee on Technology, *Preparing for the Future of Artificial Intelligence*, 2016	✓	✓		
National Security Commission on Artificial Intelligence, *Interim Report*, 2019	✓	✓	✓	✓
National Institute of Standards and Technology, *U.S. Leadership in AI: A Plan for Federal Engagement in Developing Technical Standards and Related Tools*, 2019	✓	✓		✓
President Trump, *Executive Order on Maintaining American Leadership in Artificial Intelligence*, 2019	✓			✓

Analysis of Metric Categorization

As described in Volume 1, we collected 241 metrics from 30 different Defense Advanced Research Projects Agency (DARPA) Broad Agency Announcements (BAA), during the period 2014–2020, and assessed which category each metric belonged to, if any.[5] Table 4.2 shows DARPA programs included in our analysis.

In addition to the analysis in Volume 1, we also compared findings from the expert panel on the relative importance of the solution characteristics with the results of our analysis of DARPA metric classifications to see if they were in accord. As shown in Table 4.3, the measures of performance (MoP) appearing in the greatest number of DARPA programs (i.e., soundness and optimality) differ from the solution capabilities emerging as most critical from the expert panel (i.e., robustness).

There are at least two reasons for this discrepancy. First, much of the work on AI arises from an academic tradition where accuracy metrics are used to compare the performance of systems to one another. Our category definitions of soundness and optimality (the two categories labeled as least important by the expert panel) capture most accuracy metrics from the DARPA BAAs. Second, robustness requires testing a system across a range of conditions. It is more common to demonstrate system performance in more limited cases first, which implies measures of soundness and optimality before measures of robustness.

Finally, we categorized the wording of the metrics according to whether they referred to the AI algorithm itself or to the complete system in which it was embedded. We expected MoP to predominantly apply to the AI algorithms, measures of effectiveness (MoE) to apply to both algorithms and complete systems, and measures of suitability (MoS) to predominantly apply to complete systems. As shown in Figure 4.1, this was the case.

---

[5]   Originally we considered 53 BAAs, but we narrowed it to 30 that were relevant to AI. Of the 258 metrics in these programs, 17 were judged not to be associated with AI, leaving 241 metrics. Two team members categorized all metrics separately and then reconciled their lists. There was initially a wide discrepancy in coding between the two members, which underscores the importance of clear definitions.

Table 4.2
Defense Advanced Research Projects Agency Broad Agency Announcements Retained for Analysis

Program Element	DARPA Program
Information integration systems	Composable Logistics and Information Omniscience (LogX)
Math and computer sciences	Guaranteeing AI Robustness Against Deception (GARD)
	Machine Common Sense (MCS)
	World Modelers
AI and human-machine symbiosis	Active Interpretation of Disparate Alternatives (AIDA)
	Assured Autonomy
	Explainable AI (XAI)
	Knowledge-Directed AI Reasoning over Schemas (KAIROS)
	Low Resource Languages for Emergent Incidents (LORELEI)
	Robust Automatic Transcription of Speech (RATS)
Joint warfare systems	Air Combat Evolution (ACE)
	Prototype Resilient Operations Testbed for Expeditionary Urban Scenarios (PROTEUS)
	Resilient Synchronized Planning and Assessment for the Contested Environment (RSPACE)
Maritime systems	Cross Domain Maritime Surveillance and Targeting (CDMaST)
	Ocean of Things
Naval warfare technology	Angler
Advanced land systems technology	Squad X
	Urban Reconnaissance through Supervised Autonomy (URSA)
Aeronautics technology	OFFensive Swarm-Enabled Tactics (OFFSET)
Information analytics technology	Adapting Cross-Domain Kill-Webs (ACK)
	Causal Exploration of Complex Operational Environments
	Data-Driven Discovery of Models (D3M)
	Distributed Battle Management (DBM)
	Media Forensics (MediFor)
	Warfighter Analytics Using Smartphones for Health (WASH)
Other	Context Reasoning for Autonomous Teaming (CREATE)
	Hyper-Dimensional Data Enabled Neural Networks (HyDDENN)
	Real Time Machine Learning (RTML)
	Symbiotic Design for Cyber Physical Systems
	Semantic Forensics (SemaFor)

Table 4.3
Importance of Artificial Intelligence Solution Capabilities and Measures of Performance

Ranking	Solution Capability	Percentage of MoP	Percentage of DARPA Programs with At Least One MoP in this Category
1	Robustness	10	33
2	Assured[a]	–	–
3	Learning	8	23
4	Explainability/credibility[a]	–	–
5	Data efficiency	6	17
6	Computational efficiency	14	30
7	Soundness	44	50
8	Optimality	18	53

[a] These were considered as measures of suitability (MoS).

Figure 4.1
Classification of Defense Advanced Research Projects Agency Metrics by Algorithm/System

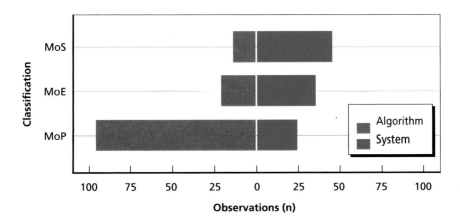

From this analysis, we see that the proposed categories of measures cover the vast majority of current metrics and appear to be reasonably well aligned to their use.

Metrics Scorecard

To aid in the development and evaluation of these three categories of measure, we offer a "scorecard" template. It is a matrix that maps measure categories to critical operational issues (COI), which are defined as follows:

> COIs are key operational effectiveness or suitability issues that must be examined . . . to determine the system's capability to perform its mission. COIs must be relevant to the required capabilities and of key importance to the system being operationally effective, operationally suitable and survivable, and represent a significant risk if not satisfactorily resolved.[6]

Figure 4.2 provides an example for an AI solution to improving the MAAP process. Here we show COI for the MAAP process and all associated metrics. Note that not all COI are associated with a metric in each category.

---

[6] DoD, *Glossary of Defense Acquisition Acronyms and Terms*, Fort Belvoir, Va.: Defense Acquisition University, 2017.

Figure 4.2
Metrics Scorecard Example for Master Air Attack Planning

Objective(s): MAAP matches available resources to the prioritized target list and accounts for air refueling requirements, suppression of enemy air defenses requirements, air defense, ISR, and other factors affecting the plan.

Measure Category		COI 1: How well does the solution allocate available resources to the target list?	COI 2: How well does the solution improve overall fleet effectiveness?	COI 3: How well does the solution operate within the existing C2 structure?
MoP	Computational efficiency	Time to generate allocation. System memory requirements.	–	–
	Data efficiency	Training dataset requirements	–	–
	Soundness	Percentage of invalid assignments	–	–
	Optimality	Comparison with best assignment (mathematical or expert judgment)	Improvement of outcomes based on modeling and simulation	–
	Robustness	Domain of algorithm (distance, time, resources)	Appropriateness of domain of algorithm to real conditions	Ability to use at different echelons, different centers
	Learning	Improvement of soundness/ optimality with additional data	–	–
MoE	Mission success	Effectiveness of allocation	Force advantage gained due to improved MAAP	–
	Survivable/ lethality	Percentage targets destroyed	Force exchange ratio	–
	Situational awareness	Additional targets detected by allocated aircraft	Decisionmaker rating of situational awareness improvement (if any)	Improvements in situational awareness at other echelons (if any)
	Timeliness	–	–	Time for larger MAAP process to be completed
	Resource management	Efficiency of allocation	–	Availability of slots for ad hoc targeting
MoS	Reducibility	Uptime	–	–
	Maintainability/ sustainability	–	–	Availability of trained personnel to fix errors
	Interoperability	–	–	Integration of solution with existing Air Operations Center systems
	Scalability	Maximum number of resources or targets solution can handle	–	Ability to expand human-machine team as use grows
	Cybersecurity	–	–	Appropriate controls for required classification level
	Human systems integration	–	–	User rating
	Explainability/ credibility	User rating	Decisionmaker trust in assessment	Decisionmaker understanding of classification

CHAPTER FIVE

Case Study 1: Master Air Attack Planning

In Chapter 2, we compared two computational solutions for developing the MAAP—a MIP technique and a GH. Based on the critical problem-solution mappings identified by the expert panel, the heuristic's capabilities appear more closely aligned with MAAP's characteristics than the mixed-integer technique. In this first technical case study, we implement both solutions to conduct a more rigorous evaluation of their suitability for MAAP.

Problem Overview

Master air attack planning is the process used to create the daily time-phased air and space scheme of maneuver—the MAAP.[1] The process involves assigning a nonhomogeneous fleet of aircraft (e.g., strike, suppression of enemy air defense, escort, tankers) stationed at various bases to flight packages (combination of aircraft working together) to execute a variety of missions. The objective is to maximize the cumulative value of completed missions by scheduling the highest priority missions and the greatest number of missions possible given the set of constrained resources.[2]

At present, master air attack planning is an extremely manpower-intensive and largely manual process. Two shifts of planners in the

---

[1] U.S. Air Force, *Operational Employment: Air Operations Center*, AFTTP 3-3 AOC, Washington, D.C., March 31, 2016. Not available to the general public.

[2] In practice, MAAP takes other objectives into account, such as maximizing aircraft survivability and conserving enough aircraft to respond to contingencies.

MAAP team work for 24 hours to develop a MAAP for each ATO cycle. The process of generating the MAAP is not particularly algorithmic—it involves gathering and discussing component priorities and leveraging human expertise to determine the best employment of air power and all-domain effects. The application of computational methods to master air attack planning could reduce planning time, increase plan quality, and free up human capital to allow planners to consider more courses of action (COAs).

Figure 5.1 shows a stylized depiction of the planning problem. Specific aircraft (i.e., tails) are stationed at different bases. A set of 50 partially planned missions are provided as inputs. These could originate from missions planned against the joint integrated prioritized target list. Planned details include mission start points and ending points, mission durations, and the package composition required for the mission. During MAAP planning, tails are assigned to packages and missions.[3] Mission packages, in turn, are assigned to anchor tracks for refueling requirements. In the model, the package marshals at the anchor, refuels if necessary, and initiates the mission. Upon completing its assigned objectives, the package egresses from the target area. We make several assumptions to increase the tractability of the model: (1) all aircraft and tankers are available for the entire time horizon; (2) tankers are assigned to one anchor track per deployment; (3) tankers can refuel any aircraft; and (4) the time required to refuel an aircraft is negligible.

A solution to the planning problem consists of the following:

1. *The set of missions to execute.* The number of potential missions may exceed the number that can be executed given limited resources.
2. *Temporal windows for each mission.* All missions must be initiated and completed within the 24-hour ATO period (for this model, though not always in reality).

---

[3] A single aircraft can complete additional missions in one ATO period but only after returning to its home station and remaining grounded for long enough to allow for maintenance, refueling, and rearming.

Figure 5.1
Master Air Attack Planning Problem Overview

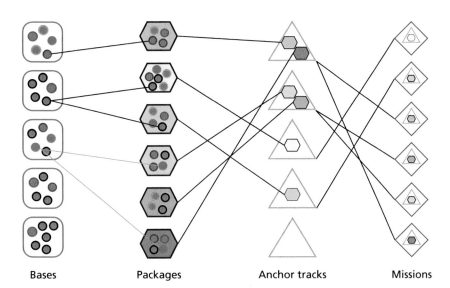

| Bases | Packages | Anchor tracks | Missions |

3. *The assignment of aircraft to packages.* Package compositions, in terms of the numbers and types of aircraft, are provided, but tails must be assigned to packages.
4. *The assignment of packages and tankers to tanker orbits (i.e., anchors).* Anchors are fixed, but the assignments of packages and tankers to those anchors are flexible.

Solutions must satisfy a set of mission constraints (e.g., the package must include all required aircraft), refueling constraints (e.g., tankers must have enough off-load capacity and aircraft must have enough fuel to complete missions and return to bases), and scheduling constraints (e.g., aircraft may be reused only after they have returned to base for maintenance, fuel, and rearming).

In sum, MAAP is a complex optimization problem (with many constraints) that is currently approached in an almost entirely manual fashion. An AI system that enabled MAAP would greatly accelerate the planning process, improve plan quality, and free up significant human capital.

System Architecture

We formulate the MAAP problem as a deterministic, mixed-integer linear program. Each mission has a value notionally derived from strategy-to-task methodology, where mission prioritization corresponds to mission criticality.[4] The quality of a plan is determined simply as the sum of the values of all scheduled missions. Mission schedules and aircraft assignments are constrained by mission execution parameters, aircraft capabilities, and aircraft utilization rates and turn times.

We looked at two different solution methods. The first is an off-the-shelf commercial solver (i.e., Gurobi) that uses integer programming theory. We refer to this method as the MIP. The second solution is the GH as described by Kevin Rossillon.[5] The GH simply schedules missions in descending order of importance (when possible) until all resources have been used or the duration of the execution window has elapsed. The MIP will always find an optimal solution (if one exists) given enough computational resources and time. The heuristic is not guaranteed to find an optimal solution or even a good one—but it will find a solution quickly.

Test Cases

We compared the two solutions using a test case described by Rossillon that involves 20 aircraft, of five different types, and four tankers.[6] Aircraft are stationed across eight bases. A list of 50 prioritized, partially planned missions, each requiring from 1 to 7 aircraft, are provided for the 24-hour ATO period. We first examined the performances of the solutions on 100 problems formed by randomly sampling ten missions from the complete test instance. We then compared the solutions on the full test instance.[7]

---

[4]   U.S. Air Force, 2016.

[5]   Rossillon, 2015.

[6]   Rossillon, 2015.

[7]   Computations were performed on a RAND computer with Intel Core i7 2.5 GHz processors and 16 GB of RAM. Gurobi 8.1.1 was utilized as the commercial solver and implement with Python 2.7.

Figure 5.2
Notional Utilities of Missions in Planning Problem

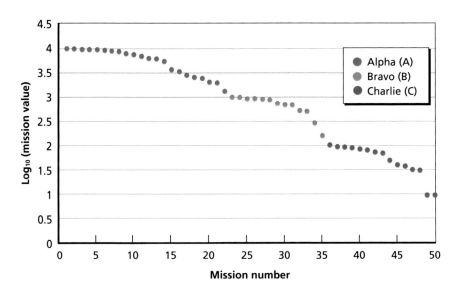

The full problem instance included 50 missions. Each mission had an associated value. Values were divided among three roughly logarithmically spaced tiers (Alpha, Bravo, and Charlie), and the values of missions within tiers varied at a more granular level (Figure 5.2).

Results

Figure 5.3 compares the solution quality and time of both the MIP and the GH based on the 100 smaller test cases. The MIP solved all instances to optimality, while the heuristic only solved 46 percent of the instances to optimality (Figure 5.3, top panel).[8] Although the MIP solved each instance to optimality, it did so at great computational cost (Figure 5.3, bottom panel). Across the 100 small test cases, the

---

[8] The MIP is needed to benchmark an optimal solution; without the MIP, it is not possible to determine the quality of the heuristic's solution.

Figure 5.3
**Solution Optimality (top) and Time (bottom) for Mixed Integer Program
and Greedy Heuristic Approaches**

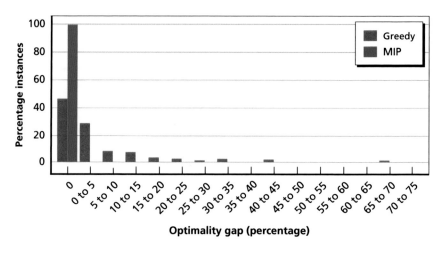

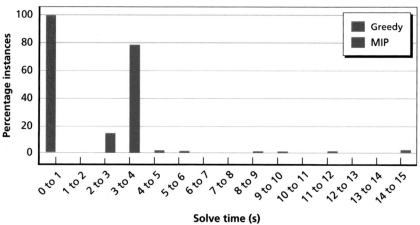

GH finds feasible (if not optimal) solutions in orders-of-magnitude less
time than the MIP.

For the full test instance, the heuristic finds a feasible solution
that comes within 17 percent of optimality after two seconds. Conversely, the MIP finds a feasible solution that comes within 2 percent
of optimality after ten hours. Figure 5.4 shows the optimality gap—

Figure 5.4
Optimality Gap as a Function of Solve Time for Mixed Integer Program and Greedy Heuristic Approaches

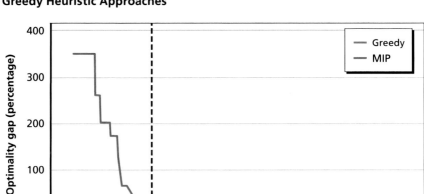

which is based on the difference between the value of the best solution yet found and the best possible value—as a function of run time. The MIP improves dramatically over the first several minutes, and it surpasses the heuristic's solution after ten minutes. Over the remaining nine-plus hours, the MIP gradually reduces the optimality gap by an additional 15 percent.

Other measures besides total operational utility are also important, for example, the number and priority of scheduled missions. Given the full set of 50 potential missions, the GH and the MIP managed to schedule a similar number of missions (GH = 31, MIP = 32). The difference in optimality gap, therefore, arose from the MIP's ability to bypass certain high-priority targets in order to service a larger number of lower-priority targets, which had greater cumulative value. Indeed, the distribution of scheduled missions across the high-, medium-, and low-priority tiers for the MIP equaled 21-7-3, whereas the distribution for the heuristic equaled 19-6-6. Even though the heuristic schedules missions in order of importance, it does not consider the resources they will use. This may lead to allocating a large percentage of resources to a mission that is only marginally more important and far more costly than others. The MIP, on the other hand, implicitly trades off mission value and cost by comparing the cumulative value of all scheduled missions rather than by prioritizing any one mission.

Another important operational outcome is tanker utilization. Although the heuristic and the MIP scheduled similar numbers of missions, the MIP utilized tankers more efficiently. On average, each tanker flight refueled 2.6 missions in the heuristic's solution versus 7.5 missions in the MIP's solution. This is because the MIP aligns the start times of missions in the same geographical regions to allow a tanker at a single anchor to refuel multiple missions. The difference in tanker utilization translates to monetary savings or, alternately, increased capacity to support additional missions.

The MIP is somewhat extensible—the same commercial solver is applicable to problem instances that include additional constraints. For example, in a communications-degraded environment, it may be preferable to create mission packages made up entirely of aircraft from one or a small number of bases. We incorporated this detail into a variant of the model as a soft constraint that penalized the objective for forming mission packages with aircraft from different bases. As shown in Table 5.1, this produced a solution that, although equivalent in value to the nonpenalized model, reduced the average number of different bases tasked per mission.

This case study demonstrates a framework for determining optimal aircraft assignments for mission scheduling subject to time, fuel, and fleet constraints. Quality solutions can be obtained using the MIP and associated commercial solver by terminating the solver after (1) a predefined amount of time is reached or (2) an optimality threshold

Table 5.1
Base Utilization in Standard and Penalized Mixed Integer Program Model

Metric	Standard Model	Penalized Model
Cumulative mission value	35,111	35,111
Average bases per mission	1.9	1.4

is achieved. Notwithstanding the high quality of its solutions, the MIP entails significant time complexity. Even for moderately sized inputs, the MIP takes hours to converge to a near-optimal solution. In theory, this time complexity is acceptable—Air Force doctrine calls for a 24-hour period for MAAP planning.[9] In practice, new inputs may become available during the 24-hour period, triggering the need for rapid replanning. Additionally, problem instances may include vastly more targets and effects, resulting in prohibitively long times for the MIP to converge.[10] An alternative approach, the GH, finds a solution of indeterminant quality, but it does so nearly instantaneously.

Given the problem characteristics embodied in MAAP, the capabilities of the MIP and the heuristic produce suitability scores of 176 and 199, respectively. In other words, the heuristic is preferred. A third possibility exists: the heuristic's solution (or the solution generated by some other intelligent system, human or artificial) can be provided to the MIP as a warm start. Such a hybrid architecture would give a rapid initial solution, and it would refine the solution as time allowed. The suitability score for the hybrid option is 200. In other words, by combining the computational efficiency of the heuristic with the optimality of the MIP, the hybrid solution is more suitable for MAAP than either of its constituent parts.

Extension of Mixed Integer Program to Multiobjective Optimization
Mission scheduling is a multiobjective optimization problem. In addition to the value of missions accomplished, planners must consider aircraft survivability, or risk. The MIP can be extended to account for risk. Specifically, we may impose predefined levels of risk for missions based on their proximity to enemy defenses or sensors. The MIP may then be constrained to find a solution that optimizes mission value subject to a specified level of risk.

---

[9]   U.S. Air Force, 2016.

[10]   In terms of the taxonomy of problem characteristics, simplifications in the first case study can be seen as limiting the problem complexity dimension. As the problem becomes more complex, the simpler heuristic might be favored to an even greater extent.

We propose a bi-objective MIP that is identical to the one implemented here save for the inclusion of a secondary objective—to optimize total mission value while minimizing total mission risk. To do so, we assign risk values to each of the 50 missions in the full set, and we use multiobjective optimization techniques (i.e., the ε-constraint method) to reformulate the secondary objective as a constraint of the model. This enables us to solve for the set of nondominated solutions along the trade-off curve. That is, we can determine the set of solutions for which neither objective (risk nor value) can be improved without degrading the other.

In this scenario, there is no single "best" solution but rather a set of solutions that are optimal given different risk limits. To solve for these points, we introduce the constraint that cumulative risk across scheduled missions remains within the specified bound. Once solved, we increase the bound on risk by a small amount ε and re-solve. To determine the entire set of nondominated solutions, we need to set ε appropriately so that no solution exists with risk level between R and $R + \varepsilon$. A potential trade-off curve is shown in Figure 5.5.

Figure 5.5
Trade-Off Between Cumulative Mission Risk and Value

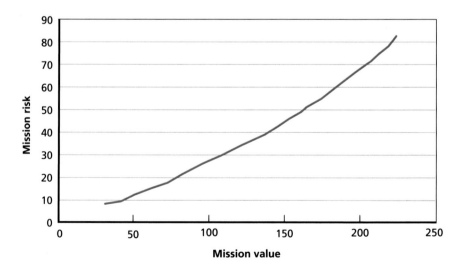

CHAPTER SIX

Case Study 2: Automatic Target Recognition with Learning

Our comparison of games and C2 processes in Volume 1 showed that more problem characteristics were present—and more pronounced—in C2 processes than in games. In particular, all C2 processes involve environmental clutter/noise and incomplete information. Results from the expert panel established that these problem characteristics jointly call for two solution capabilities: robustness and learning. Yet this combination of capabilities, robustness (against sensory noise) and learning, may be difficult to achieve in practice: RL agents have empirically been shown to require extensive training to master even simple behaviors in noisy environments.[1] Given that noise is a pervasive characteristic of C2 processes, RL approaches that can handle noise are of great interest.

In this second technical case study, we explore the use of a closed-loop sensing algorithm to mitigate the effects of noise on a learning agent using an artificial environment, *StarCraft II*. In the system architecture we propose, the closed-loop sensing algorithm acts as a modular processing tool that an RL agent can learn to use. We demonstrate the architecture using a notional example of sensor management.

---

[1] Mark Pendrith, *On Reinforcement Learning of Control Actions in Noisy and Non-Markovian Domains*, University of New South Wales, Sydney, UNSW-CSE TR-9410, 1994.

Environment

StarCraft II is a real-time strategy game in which a player controls futuristic military and support units for harvesting resources and attacking enemy forces. A single game involves multiple human players and constructive agents. The action space is exceptionally large and, compared with other games, rich with hierarchical structure.[2] This makes *StarCraft II* more comparable to real C2 processes than other games, such as chess and Texas Hold'em. Yet the default *StarCraft II* environment remains limited in two ways:

1. In the default environment, rewards are given for destroying an enemy player or for collecting resources. Active sensing could contribute to the attainment of these goals, but we were interested in studying sensing behavior in isolation.
2. The default *StarCraft II* environment does not include substantial environmental noise.

To overcome these limitations, we made two changes to the default *StarCraft II* environment. First, we defined a new function that rewarded the agent for making five or more consecutive correct classifications of a ground unit. This encouraged sustained tracking behavior. After the agent reached more than ten consecutive correct classifications of one ground unit, a larger reward became available for exploring other ground units. Second, we introduced the notion of a range-dependent sensor aboard an airborne platform. As distance from ground units increased, the sensor's accuracy decreased, according to a half-Gaussian distribution. This introduced the need for the agent to learn where to position the airborne unit to improve classification accuracy.

To model environmental noise in *StarCraft II*, we assumed that the performance of the sensor aboard the observing platform is range dependent—in effect, range becomes the relevant performance param-

---

2   Oriol Vinyals, Timo Ewalds, Sergey Bartunov, Petko Georgiev, Alexander Sasha Vezhnevets, Michelle Yeo, Alireza Makhzani, Heinrich Küttler, John Agapiou, Julian Schrittwieser et al., "StarCraft II: A New Challenge for Reinforcement Learning," Ithaca, N.Y.: Cornell University, eprint arxiv:1708.04782, August 2017.

Figure 6.1
Noisy Sensor Classification Accuracy Profile

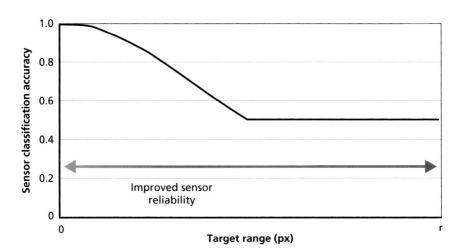

eter that drives the selection of actions in closed-loop automatic target recognition (CL-ATR). The range dependence, *r*, is modeled with a half-Gaussian distribution as shown in Figure 6.1, where a correct classification is provided with a 50 percent probability at large in-game pixel distances.[3] Additionally, unit ownership (friend, foe, or neutral), a default tag provided by the *StarCraft II* application programming interface (API), was masked to force the agent to base classifications on sensor inputs only.

Additional mathematical details about the reward function may be found in Appendix B.

System Architectures

Closed-Loop Automatic Target Recognition
CL-ATR is a form of automatic target recognition in which an agent attempts to improve the quality of the information provided to a

---

[3] The sensor abstraction used in the simulation could be replaced by a high-fidelity model of a physical sensor along with its relative performance parameters.

classification algorithm by optimally adjusting such parameters as sensor placement. CL-ATR may also be understood as a version of active vision, except that it is not limited to the visual modality, and, conversely, it only aims to solve an automatic target recognition problem.[4] One implementation of CL-ATR is shown in Figure 6.2.[5]

The algorithm assumes a pretrained classifier whose performance profile with respect to parameters of interest is known in advance and is represented as a set of confusion matrices. A typical parameter configuration might include the pose of a sensor—range, azimuth, and elevation—relative to a detected target whose class is to be ascertained. In the case of an image sensor, other parameters might include zoom

Figure 6.2
Closed-Loop Automatic Target Recognition Implementation

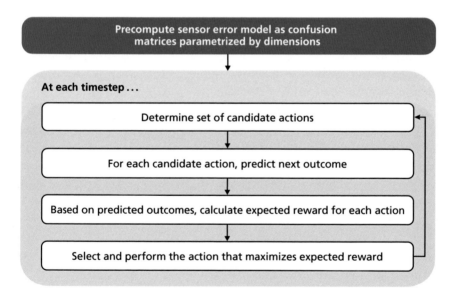

---

[4]   Dana H. Ballard, "Animate Vision," *Artificial Intelligence*, Vol. 48, No. 1, 1991.

[5]   Ssu-Hsin Yu, Pat McLaughlin, Aleksandar Zatezalo, Kai-yuh Hsiao, and J. Boskovic, "Integrate Knowledge Acquisition with Target Recognition Through Closed-Loop ATR," *Proceedings of Signal Processing, Sensor/Information Fusion, and Target Recognition XXIV*, Vol. 9474, 2015.

level, image brightness and contrast, and spectral band. Confusion matrices are computed from empirical measurements at a fixed number of points in the parameter configuration space—for example, at different ranges, azimuths, and elevations to the target. Simple interpolation is used to extend the confusion matrix to points not included in the sampled configuration space.

At run time, CL-ATR cycles through the steps in Figure 6.2. The algorithm begins by identifying all potential actions. Next, it uses the confusion matrices to predict the observations expected for each potential action. Based on the predicted observations, the algorithm calculates the expected reward for each potential action. Reward is quantified in terms of the decrease in entropy or, alternatively, the information gain associated with the expected observation. Finally, the algorithm selects and implements the action with the highest expected reward.

Despite its simplicity, CL-ATR performs well compared with more complex Bayesian filtering approaches.[6] CL-ATR is also extremely flexible; for example, it can be extended to multiple-step look-ahead planning with multiple agents, as well as target detection prior to target recognition. Finally, CL-ATR can be used as part of a larger AI system architecture.

Asynchronous Advantage Actor-Critic

The Asynchronous Advantage Actor-Critic (A3C) algorithm is a model-free, on-policy RL algorithm, in which the agent does not attempt to model the transition function between states or the reward function associated with the environment (Figure 6.3).[7] Rather, A3C learns an action policy (an *actor*) that is scored by a value prediction (a *critic*). The term *advantage* refers to an estimate of the value function that provides critic feedback (δ) to the actor. The *asynchronous* aspect of A3C relates to the parallel nature of the algorithm, where

---

[6]   T. Arbel and F. P. Ferrie, "On the Sequential Accumulation of Evidence," *International Journal of Computer Vision*, Vol. 43, 2001.

[7]   V. Mnih, A. P. Badia, M. Mirza, A. Graves, T. Lillicrap, T. Harley, D. Silver, and K. Kavukcuoglu, "Asynchronous Methods for Deep Reinforcement Learning," *Proceedings of the 33rd International Conference on Machine Learning*, Vol. 48, 2016.

Figure 6.3
Single Worker Instance in Asynchronous Advantage Actor-Critic Architecture

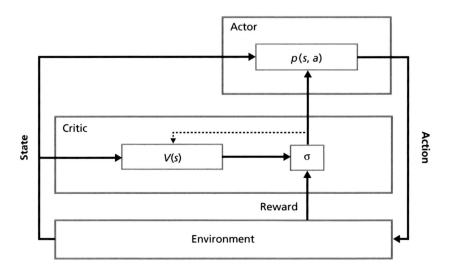

several agent workers are dispatched simultaneously to explore, sample, and train locally. The pool of workers asynchronously contributes their learned experiences to a global policy. This allows the global policy to benefit from the diversity of the ensemble of workers.

We trained the A3C agent in a modified *StarCraft II* game environment. The environment provides spatial and nonspatial inputs to the agent. When applied to *StarCraft II*, the A3C architecture is structured to accept spatial information through several successive two-dimensional convolutional layers, while nonspatial information is introduced into the network through several dense layers. Ultimately, information is reduced and combined into additional dense layers that output a value estimate for the current state (i.e., the critic) and a probabilistic decision for nonspatial and spatial actions (i.e., the actor). The training in the *StarCraft II* environment is performed using 20 workers on an Amazon Web Services instance.[8]

---

[8]   The parameters used for training the A3C agent across all cases in this analysis are shown in Appendix B.

Closed-Loop Automatic Target Recognition as an Expert in a Reinforcement Learning System

This work explores the integration of CL-ATR with an RL paradigm. To do so, we treated CL-ATR as a type of expert that recommends optimal sensing actions (i.e., ship positions) to the A3C agent at each time step. The A3C agent then decides whether to follow CL-ATR recommendations versus selecting from other spatial actions. Effectively, this shifts the target of learning from a low-level sensing policy (which is now provided by CL-ATR) to a high-level control policy. Because CL-ATR incorporates prior knowledge about sensor performance in its model, the integration of CL-ATR with A3C in this way may accelerate learning. Additionally, the A3C agent can generalize the learned high-level control policy to different sensors by merely changing the confusion matrices given to CL-ATR. Finally, the design pattern can be repurposed by incorporating other modular, model-based experts into the system architecture (e.g., an evasive-maneuver recommender) and by training the A3C agent to learn which experts to listen to and in which circumstances.

Test Cases

In this environment, the agent controls an airborne platform. Its task is to position itself so as to assign friend or foe classifications to two mobile ground units (Figure 6.4). The agent is evaluated using a two-by-two factorial design. The first factor is whether sensor noise was present. The second factor is whether the A3C agent was given access to the CL-ATR positional recommendations.

Agent performance is measured in terms of time on station (TOS)—that is, the number of consecutive game frames (up to a maximum of 10) assigning the correct label to a ground target. Each episode included two ground targets, so the maximum score for TOS was 20.

In the absence of sensor noise, we hypothesized that CL-ATR would not produce a significant advantage. In the presence of sensor noise, we hypothesized that the agent would require more training, but this could be mitigated by the inclusion of CL-ATR.

Figure 6.4
Initial Setup of *StarCraft II* Observing Platform and Targets with Patrols

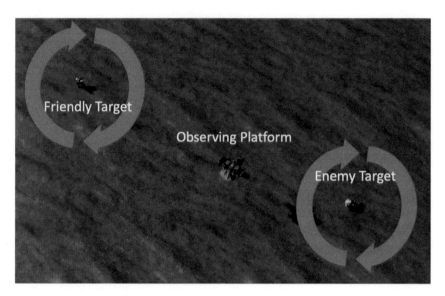

SOURCE: Blizzard *STARCRAFT II* Map Editor.

We trained the A3C agent in four scenarios corresponding to the cross of sensor noise (absent, present) and CL-ATR (absent, present). All four cases were run with 20 workers given a maximum number of 100 time steps. This corresponds to 4.8 minutes of game play. The screen was repositioned to center the observing platform every 10 time steps, and the agent made in-game steps after every eight frames.

The *StarCraft II* Python API returns the screen and minimap for every environment agent time step both with image sizes of 32 by 32 pixels. Training episodes were performed on *StarCraft II* map containing no terrain obstacles and two targets, one friendly and one foe. The two targets performed deterministic circular overlapping patrols. At the start of each episode, the observing platform was spawned between the two targets.

In the noisy sensor training, the sensor profile uses a range distance of $r = 5$ pixels to set the threshold where targets have a classification accuracy of 50 percent for $r \geq 5$ and 50–100 percent for $r < 5$.

Results

Experiment results are shown in Figure 6.5. When sensor noise was absent, pure A3C (blue) and A3C with CL-ATR (red) performed equally well.[9] Both agents approached near maximum performance (i.e., TOS = 20) after about 50 hours of training. When sensor noise was present, pure A3C (orange) failed to learn to observe both targets after 200 hours of training (i.e., TOS < 10). A3C with CL-ATR (green), in contrast, learned to observe both targets, albeit at a slower rate than with a noiseless sensor (i.e., TOS > 10).

This case study explores the use of CL-ATR to deal with environmental clutter/noise and incomplete information, two pervasive characteristics of C2 problems. We used CL-ATR to provide expert

Figure 6.5
Comparison Between Training Cases Under Ideal and Noisy Sensor Conditions

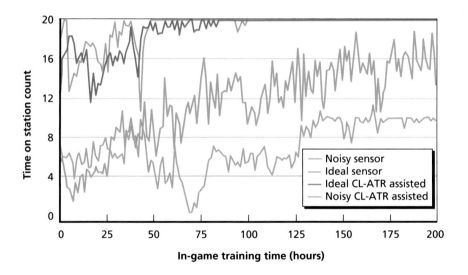

---

[9] Pure A3C achieves the maximum level of performance somewhat sooner because the size of its input space is smaller due to the omission of the CL-ATR component, facilitating training. This is beneficial in the noiseless environment but not the noisy environment.

recommendations, which the A3C agent learned to use. This proved necessary for learning in the noisy environment.

Extension to Air Battle Manager Sensor Management

Our test case involved an airborne unit sensing two ground units, but the AI system could be used to sense other airborne units as well. To define this potential extension, we describe the sensor management task performed by an Air Surveillance Officer (ASO) aboard an E-3 AWACS, and we briefly consider the potential for applying A3C with CL-ATR to that task. This technical approach is also applicable elsewhere, for example, to sensor brokering in the Advanced Battle Management System.

The E-3 AWACS is an element of the tactical air control system, the Air Force's mechanism for commanding and controlling airpower.[10] Responsibility as the region or sector air defense commander may be decentralized to AWACS, which acts as the primary integration point for air defense fighters and fire control in its assigned area.

The E-3's ASO manages a team to detect, identify, monitor, and report friendly, hostile, and potentially hostile airborne and maritime tracks; the ASO also coordinates with other surveillance teams throughout the theater, to ensure a common operational picture. The surveillance team operates and manages active and passive sensors and tactical data links and performs identification functions. The three primary concerns for the ASO and surveillance team are (1) getting optimum performance from both active and passive sensors, (2) communicating onboard and off-board tracks with other surveillance stations in the assigned area of responsibility for an optimum common picture, and (3) meeting mission requirements by handling tactical issues that force deviations from the planned mission. To optimize sensor performance, the ASO and surveillance team may select from a wide range of actions involving which sensors, modes, orientations, and azimuths to employ. Additionally, the ASO and surveillance team can make recommendations regarding tactical orbits to optimize sensor performance.

---

[10] U.S. Air Force Doctrine, "Appendix D: Theater Air Control System," in *Annex 3-30: Command and Control*, Maxwell Air Force Base, Ala.: Lemay Center for Doctrine, 2020c.

The *StarCraft II* example, though much simpler than the ASO's sensor management task, nonetheless shares several functional features of that task, namely, the real-time selection of sensing actions to maximize information gain. Table 6.1 enumerates additional features of the ASO task, along with suggestions for how the AI system presented in this case study could be expanded to accommodate them.

Table 6.1
Potential Extensions of Asynchronous Advantage Actor-Critic with Closed-Loop Automatic Target Recognition for Air Surveillance Officer Sensor Management

ASO Sensor Management	Extension to CL-ATR
AWACS is equipped with a multitude of sensors with different modes. Sensor performance is affected by a multitude of environmental and employment parameters.	Generate confusion matrices for all sensors, modes, and parameters.
Sensors and modes may be employed in sequences.	Extend CL-ATR to multistep look-ahead and action selection.
AWACS is in communication with other partially independent airborne and ground-based sensing nodes.	Extend CL-ATR to multiagent planning.
Certain actions, such as orbit selection, must take into account other constraints beyond sensor returns (i.e., fuel consumption, range, threat avoidance).	Extend the evaluative function used in CL-ATR for action selection.
The ASO receives an intelligence briefing prior to mission execution. This includes information about adversary order of battle and disposition.	Include information priors (i.e., expectations) in CL-ATR corresponding to expected adversary locations and identities.
The battle space includes complex terrain and effects.	Extend the *StarCraft II* environment to represent the features and their effects on sensor and task performance.
After identifying a track, the ASO must monitor its behavior.	Extend the AI system to include memory of labeled tracks and to periodically shift attention back to each.
The ASO must communicate relevant information to consumers.	Extend the AI system to infer the importance of track labels and behaviors to different agents and to minimize extraneous communications.

CHAPTER SEVEN

Case Study 3: Human-Machine Teaming for Personnel Recovery

The previous two case studies focused on "pure" AI and computational architectures. Yet DoD reports and directives repeatedly emphasize that AI will not supplant humans. Rather, humans will remain an integral part of human-machine teams.[1] In this technical case study, we consider a mixed-initiative system for personnel recovery (PR). This is exceptionally demanding in many ways: PR has high operational tempo, high operational risks and benefits, a large percentage of incomplete information, and a near absence of historical data for training. Given this constellation of problem characteristics, a hybrid architecture with human and machine intelligence may be most suitable for PR planning.

The AI component of the mixed-initiative system involves a game theory construct. Properties of game theory models are well established, and components of this framework can be mapped onto components of C2 processes. For example, Table 7.1 presents standard game theory terms alongside an archetypal example for studying game theory models (Texas Hold'em) and a C2 process (joint operational planning).[2,3]

[1] John Shanahan, "Artificial Intelligence Initiatives," statement to the Senate Armed Services Committee Subcommittee on Emerging Threats and Capabilities, Washington, D.C., U.S. Senate, March 12, 2019; Zacharias, 2019.

[2] E. Rasmusen, *Games and Information: An Introduction to Game Theory*, Oxford: Blackwell, 1989.

[3] Joint Publication 5-0, *Joint Operation Planning*, Washington, D.C.: U.S. Joint Chiefs of Staff, 2017.

Table 7.1
Game Theory and Course of Action Development Terms of Reference

Game Theory Terms	Texas Hold'em Poker	COA Development Terms
Players	Players	Forces/capabilities required, adversary
Payout/utility	Winning hands, prize money	Objectives, purpose
Actions	Bidding, raising, calling	Key tasks
Static/dynamic game	Sequential play	Sequencing, decision points
Perfect/imperfect information	Displayed cards, "hole" cards	Intel prep of the operating environment
Player types	Purposes for not folding	Friendly/adversary objectives and purpose
Strategy (pure or mixed)	Bluffing	COA, decisive point(s)

The mixed-initiative system we explore takes into consideration a noncooperative adversary, it integrates topical subject-matter expertise with AI, and it efficiently explores a complex solution space.

System Architecture

Every game that is composed of a finite number of moves, players, and possible actions has at least one Nash equilibrium. A Nash equilibrium represents a set of strategies, one for each player, from which no rational player could deviate to improve their outcome, assuming all players are rational.

Even with this information in mind, multistage games with many potential actions per player are difficult to resolve conventionally (using backward induction, whereby the best outcome for the last decision is determined, followed in succession by all preceding decisions by each player, back to the first). The difficulty stems from two challenges. First, the strategy solution space grows exponentially with the number of players, stages, and actions. Second, in real-world problems, some or all players may have incomplete information. In that case, the rational player must consider all possible values of concealed variables when choosing an action.

An alternate approach to an exponentially expanding decision tree is the use of influence networks. This is a probabilistic model of causality, applicable in complex situations, that relies on Bayesian updates to the probability of a given action at each step in a dynamic model or game.[4] One such model is depicted in Figure 7.1.

In this game model,[5] three variables describe the state of the world at the start of the game. These variables each influence the potential actions taken by Red and Blue in the first round. These actions are resource limited, in that not every combination may be feasible. Examples of resource limitations are personnel, consumables, or money. Three

Figure 7.1
Generic Multistage Game

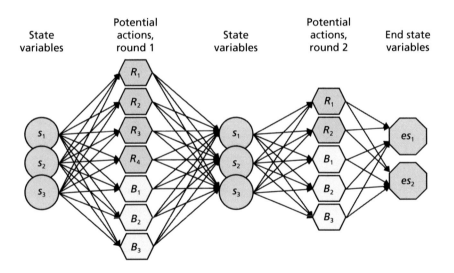

---

[4] Bayesian probability is also called *conditional probability*. This is the probability of some future action or state of the world taking place *given that some preceding event or state of the world has occurred*.

[5] For this model, we adapted the dynamic game of complete information established by Zhengjun Du, Chao Chen and Defeng Kong. See Zhengjun Du, Chao Chen, and Defeng Kong, "Modeling and Development of Course of Action by Considering Uncertainty and Antagonism," *Military Operations Research*, Vol. 19, No. 2, 2014.

additional variables describe the state of the world at the start of the second round, which influence the potential actions taken by Red and Blue in that round. The actions taken by Red and Blue in the second round influence the game's end states.

The interaction between each element of the initial state vector $\{s_1, s_2, s_3\}$ and each potential first round action $\{R_1, R_2, R_3, R_4, B_1, B_2, B_3\}$ is quantified in two measures: strength of causality (h) and strength of negation (g). These measures are represented by the directional arrows connecting states and actions in Figure 7.1. In brief, causal strengths are used to determine the probability that certain actions for Red and Blue, given current state values, will be successfully completed *if selected*. Additionally, causal strengths are used to determine the probability that future states will take certain values given the set of actions that are successfully completed by Red and Blue.

Determining Causal Strength

Strength of causality (h) is the extent to which the occurrence of a node A results in another node B subsequently occurring. Relatedly, strength of negation (g) is the extent to which the absence of a node A results in another node B subsequently occurring. Strength of negation and causality are bounded by −1 and 1. If $h = 1$, the presence of A leads to B's occurrence with 100 percent certainty. If $h = -1$, the absence of A leads to B's occurrence with 100 percent certainty. If $h = 0$, A has no effect on B. Similarly, if $g = 1$, the presence of A leads to B's nonoccurrence with 100 percent certainty. If $g = -1$, the absence of A leads to B's nonoccurrence with 100 percent certainty. If $g = 0$, the absence of A has no effect on B.

In the absence of historical or simulator data, causal strength values are estimated by SMEs. To simplify determination of causal strength, the following semantically anchored definitions were provided: low = 0.3, medium = 0.6, and high = 0.9. For strength of causation, a positive value indicated that the occurrence of A enables B. For strength of negation, a positive value indicated that the absence of A enables B.

The complete set of causal strength values generated during an interview with a PR SME are displayed in Tables 7.2 through 7.5. The value at the intersection of a row and column is the likelihood of the

Table 7.2
Round 1 Strength of Causation and Negation Matrices on Action Success

Directionality	States	Actions						
		R_1	R_2	R_3	R_4	B_1	B_2	B_3
Causation	s_1	-0.9	0	0	-0.9	0.6	0	0
Causation	s_2	0	0.9	0.3	0.6	-0.3	0.9	0
Causation	s_3	0	0.3	0.3	0.9	0.9	0.9	0.9
Negation	s_1	0.9	-0.9	0	0.9	-0.6	0.3	0
Negation	s_2	0.9	-0.9	0.6	0.9	-0.6	0.9	0
Negation	s_3	0	0	0	0	0.9	0.6	-0.9

Table 7.3
Round 1 Strength of Causation and Negation Matrices on State Values

Directionality	Actions	States		
		s_1	s_2	s_3
Causation	R_1	-0.9	0	0.3
Causation	R_2	0	0.9	0
Causation	R_3	0	0	0.3
Causation	R_4	-0.6	0	-0.3
Causation	B_1	0	0	0.6
Causation	B_2	0	0	0
Causation	B_3	0	0	0.9
Negation	R_1	0.9	0.3	0.3
Negation	R_2	0	-0.9	0
Negation	R_3	0	-0.6	0
Negation	R_4	0.9	0.9	0
Negation	B_1	0	0.3	0
Negation	B_2	0	0	0
Negation	B_3	0	0	-0.9

Table 7.4
Round 2 Strength of Causation and Negation Matrices on Action Success

Directionality	States	Actions				
		R_1	R_2	B_1	B_2	B_3
Causation	s_1	0.3	0.6	0.9	0.6	0.9
Causation	s_2	−0.9	−0.9	0.3	−0.9	−0.3
Causation	s_3	0	0.3	0.9	0.9	0.9
Negation	s_1	0	0	−0.6	−0.3	−0.3
Negation	s_2	0.6	0.6	−0.3	0.6	0.9
Negation	s_3	−0.9	−0.9	−0.6	−0.6	0

Table 7.5
Round 2 Strength of Causation and Negation Matrices on State Values

Directionality	Actions	es_1	es_2
Causation	R_1	−0.6	−0.9
Causation	R_2	−0.6	0
Causation	B_1	0.3	0
Causation	B_2	0.9	0
Causation	B_3	0	0.9
Negation	R_1	0.3	0.3
Negation	R_2	0.9	0
Negation	B_1	−0.6	0
Negation	B_2	−0.9	0
Negation	B_3	0	−0.9

column variable occurring given that the row variable occurs. For example, the upper left element of the first matrix in Round 1 below corresponds to the statement "Red is highly unlikely [−0.9] to success-fully deploy CAPs near the site [R_1], given Blue has air superiority over the JOA [s_1]."

To determine the probability of any node's successful occurrence, the strengths of negation and causality from each predecessor are aggregated mathematically to update the previously expected probability using Bayes's theorem.[6] By replicating this update multiple times, the probability of achieving some end state can be calculated. In our example game above, the first round of actions updates the state elements, which in turn influence the second round of actions (again, as available, subject to resource constraints). Finally, the second round of actions influences the two-element end state $\{es_1, es_2\}$. A payoff, or utility value, can be defined as a function of the end state, and these payoffs can be compared for all feasible resource-constrained strategies.

When payoffs for all end states, and by extension for all strategies, are known, game theory analysis can identify the Nash equilibrium strategies for Red and Blue players. If a single equilibrium point for Red and/or Blue gives the best payoff, this is a *pure strategy*. If multiple Nash equilibria exist, the best approach for that player is a *mixed strategy*. If a mixed strategy equilibrium exists, that player must choose among the options in a way that makes the opposing player indifferent to their own strategy.

Assessing the strengths of causality and negation between pairs of elements in a game model is an art—and the crux of this analytic approach. Each arrow in Figure 7.1 represents where values for strength of causation and negation are required. These values may be determined from historical data, stochastic modeling, or some other method. Of relevance here, we can rely on the judgment of SMEs to compile a table of values for future use. In this way, human subject-matter expertise is inserted into an AI system.

---

[6] For a more rigorous mathematical discussion of influence networks, see Julie A. Rosen and Wayne L. Smith, "Influence Net Modeling with Causal Strengths: An Evolutionary Approach," *Military Operations Research Society*, Vol. 33, No. 4, December 2000; and Abbas K. Zaidi, Faisal Mansoor, and Titsa P. Papantoni-Kazakos, "Theory of Influence Networks," *Journal of Intelligent and Robotic Systems*, Vol. 60, No. 3–4, 2010.

Test Case

To provide a concrete example of this method, we use PR as the object of an operational planning event, and we focus on the planning and execution functions of PR.[7]

In this scenario, a friendly (Blue) aircrew has not checked in with C2 elements after flying a routine signals intelligence patrol over sparsely populated nonfriendly (Red) territory. Space-based infrared satellites spot a brief spike in energy in the vicinity of the patrol, then no further returns. The joint force commander has declared an isolated personnel (IP) event and directs the PR coordination cell to prescribe COAs. As the planning team comes together, national technical means verify an intermittent but verified locator beacon signal from the location of the infrared event. While the Red leadership are not happy with the intrusion, they have privately signaled they will not interfere with search-and-rescue air operations. The joint forces commander wants PR to remain the highest priority but also wants the sensitive signals intelligence equipment, which was on board, to be either destroyed or secured as a secondary objective. Tables 7.6 and 7.7 assign action and state definitions to nodes in the network.

For the scenario described above, we can assign the initial state values as such: $\{s_1 = 1, s_2 = 1,$ and $s_3 = 1\}$. Given these variables, a strategy for Red across two rounds of play might be represented in shorthand as: $\{r_{1,1} = 0, r_{1,2} = 0, r_{1,3} = 1, r_{1,4} = 1; r_{2,1} = 1, r_{2,2} = 0\}$. A 0 means the action is not selected, and a 1 means the action is chosen. The implication is that Red and Blue both have 2^6 (64) potential strategies available to them.

Because even the highest priority real-world missions are almost always constrained by resource availability, these model strategies are resource constrained as well. This is done in two steps. First, all actions are assigned a required number of units of consumable resources corresponding to personnel, fuel, and equipment. Second, each player has been allotted a budget of resources to apply against potential actions. This results in a final subset of viable strategies composed of only those

---

[7]   U.S. Air Force Doctrine, Annex 3-50, *Personnel Recovery*, Maxwell Air Force Base, Ala.: Lemay Center for Doctrine, 2020b.

Table 7.6
Personnel Recovery Actions

Round	Actor	Action Variables
1	Red	R_1: Deploy CAPs near site
1	Red	R_2: Negotiate with Blue for IP return
1	Red	R_3: Alert Red citizens in vicinity
1	Red	R_4: Create no-fly zone near IP site
1	Blue	B_1: Deploy ISR unmanned aerial vehicles
1	Blue	B_2: Mobilize recovery teams
1	Blue	B_3: Establish regular comm with IP
2	Red	R_1: Degrade GPS signals near IP
2	Red	R_2: Degrade communication near IP
2	Blue	B_1: Resupply IP as necessary
2	Blue	B_2: Neutralize threats to IP
2	Blue	B_3: Secure/destroy sensitive hardware

Table 7.7
Personnel Recovery States

Elements	State Variables
Battlefield state	s_1: Blue side has air superiority over Joint Operational Area
Battlefield state	s_2: Red country is cooperative
Battlefield state	s_3: IP is broadcasting position
End state	es_1: IP is secured
End state	es_2: Sensitive hardware/equipment secured

provisioned actions. Applying an arbitrary initial set of resource constraints, Red has 27 viable strategies, and Blue has 30.

The most unique element of this game theory approach is also the most difficult to produce. As noted earlier, the strength of causation and of negation for every pairing of state and action variables (Red and

Blue) is needed to ultimately resolve the end states. Example sources of these strength values are historical data, intelligence collection, or aggregated input from SMEs. To facilitate this notional example, a simplified formula was used to build the matrices of causal strengths. The formula rules and full set of values in matrix form are provided in Tables 7.2 through 7.4. The essential role of the human analyst in this hybrid architecture is to complete these values.

Finally, to attribute a payoff for each potential strategy combination, we define the Blue (friendly) utility function as: *Utility* = 0.8 × es_1 + 0.2 × es_2. This can be interpreted to mean "returning the IP is 4 times as important as securing the sensitive hardware on the aircraft."

Results

Using all this information, we resolve the game to determine Nash equilibria strategies for Red and Blue. The result for the baseline scenario is that a mixed strategy is optimal for both players. In the case of COA selection, the probabilities associated with a mixed strategy can be interpreted as the distribution among multiple viable options. For Red, the strategy mix is 66.3 percent for one strategy and 33.7 percent for another. These strategies translate as follows:

- In the first round, create a no-fly zone near the IP site. In the second round, degrade satellite communication in the vicinity of the IP (66.3 percent).
- In the first round, negotiate with Blue to return IP and alert Red citizens in the vicinity. In the second round, degrade satellite communication in the vicinity of the IP (33.7 percent).

For Blue, the strategy mix is 33.2 percent for one strategy and 66.8 percent for another. These strategies translate as follows:

- In the first round, mobilize recovery teams. In the second round, neutralize threats to the IP (33.2 percent).
- In the first round, deploy ISR unmanned aerial vehicles and establish regular communication with the IP. In the second round, secure or destroy sensitive hardware (66.8 percent).

Variations on Baseline Scenario and Results

We also considered variations on the baseline scenario that manipulated the resources available to Red and Blue or that included uncontested actions. Table 7.8 summarizes the variations and their results.

Table 7.8
Alternate Personnel Recovery Test Cases

Data Set	Red Strategies	Blue Strategies	Notes
Baseline	0001-10 66.3% 0110-10 33.7%	010-010 33.2% 101-001 66.8%	Resource constraints resulted in 27 Red and 30 Blue viable strategies.
Reduced resource	0001-10 67.5% 0100-01 32.5%	001-001 68.5% 010-010 31.5%	Reduced a single Blue resource 57% in Round 1; Reduced a single Red resource 38% in Round 2. All other conditions unchanged. (Red reduced to 18 viable strategies and Blue reduced to 15 viable strategies)
Unconstrained resources (Red and Blue)	0001-10 19.8% 0110-10 80.2%	010-010 33.1% 101-001 33.5% 111-001 33.5%	Red and Blue not resource constrained. Red had 45 viable strategies. Blue had 49 viable strategies. For realism and to reduce computational complexity, no strategies included where either player made no actions in either round (0000-xx, xxxx-00, 000-xxx, xxx-000).
Blue uncontested w/ unconstrained resources (Red unresourced)	0000-00 100%	001-001 33.3% 010-001 33.3% 011-001 33.3%	Represents Blue uncontested strategy.
Unconstrained Blue resources (Red unresourced and no strength of causality/ negation)	0000-00 100%	010-100 100%	A refinement to previous data set, removing influence of "choosing to do nothing."

Discussion

This third technical case study presents a mixed-initiative system architecture. PR instances, because of their relative rareness, are unique. The lack of historical or simulator data, the case-specific definitions of states and actions, and the multidimensional and subjective nature of outcomes resist a "pure" AI solution. The approach we present leverages multiple sources of human knowledge for (1) defining problem states, (2) defining actions, (3) assigning causal strengths between states and actions, (4) defining end states, and (5) assigning relative importance to different end states. The approach also leverages AI to apply a Bayesian updating procedure along with a method for identifying equilibria points to determine the optimal actions, given the problem specification provided by the human SME.

Table 7.9 compares the two candidate solution architectures: human alone and human plus AI. The suitability of the hybrid architecture exceeds the suitability of the human alone (192 versus 138).

The difference in suitability scores can be traced to the capabilities of the potential systems:

- *Computational efficiency.* Given time constraints, human planners can consider, at most, a very limited number of COAs. The causal network efficiently considers all COAs, increasing computational efficiency. Yet the specification of network parameters is time consuming.
- *Soundness and optimality.* The causal network will find sound and optimal solutions subject to the quality of the human experts' specification of the PR problem.
- *Robustness.* A small change to model assumptions may greatly reduce the quality of human-generated COAs. Given its computational efficiency, an approach like a causal network can generate solutions conditional on sources of uncertainty in model specification.

A limitation of the computational architecture is that it treats the adversary as being perfectly rational. Future work could replace this assumption with one of bounded rationality by using approaches like quantal response equilibrium or cognitive models to represent suboptimal adversary decisionmaking.

Table 7.9
Suitability of a Human and Mixed Architecture for Personnel Recovery

Problem Characteristic	Solution Capability	Computational Efficiency	Data Efficiency	Soundness	Optimality	Robustness	Learning	Explainability	Assuredness	
	Rating	0, 1	3, 3	2, 4	2, 4	2, 2	0, 0	3, 3	2, 4	
Operational tempo	3	0, 3		6, 12		6, 6			6, 12	
Rate of environment change	1	0, 1	3, 3			2, 2	0, 0			
Problem complexity	2	0, 2	6, 6			4, 4	0, 0	6, 6	4, 8	
Reducibility	1								2, 4	
Data availability	4		12, 12			8, 8	0, 0		8, 16	
Environmental clutter/noise	2					4, 4	0, 0		4, 8	
Stochasticity of action outcomes	0					0, 0			0, 0	
Clarity of goals and utility	0					0, 0	0, 0	0, 0		
Incompleteness of information	3		9, 9			6, 6	0, 0	9, 9		
Operational risks and benefits	3			6, 12	6, 12	6, 6		9, 9	6, 12	
Human total	0	30	12	6	36	0	24	30	138	
Human + AI total	6	30	24	12	36	0	24	60	192	

NOTE: The first value in each cell is for human, and the second value in each cell is for human plus AI.

Artificial Intelligence History

The seemingly sudden leaps in AI are a result of the steady accumulation of progress in multiple areas and, at times, relatively modest changes to algorithms and system architectures. Take, for instance, the growth of capability evident in computer chess (Figure A.1). Claude Shannon's classic paper of 1950 proposed an implementable algorithm—minimax—that was the basis of the earliest chess programs.[1] Minimax used brute-force search to a certain depth along with a heuristic to select the best considered move. In the mid-1950s, several researchers independently discovered alpha-beta pruning, a variant on the minimax algorithm that terminated the search of exploitable lines of play, allowing for a deeper exploration of stronger lines. For the next 50 years, alpha-beta pruning remained at the heart of the most powerful chess programs. During that time, increasingly powerful computers elevated the play of chess programs from amateur to grandmaster levels. IBM's chess-playing computer Deep Blue, which defeated Gary Kasparov in 1997, worked basically the same way as the programs of the 1950s, albeit with more sophisticated heuristics and the opportunity to exploit much greater computation.

In the 2010s, research on the game of Go inspired the development of a search algorithm called AlphaZero that combined DRL and MCTS. This approach depended on two things: independent research

---

[1] C. E. Shannon, "Programming a Computer for Playing Chess," *Philosophical Magazine*, Vol. 41, 1950.

Figure A.1
Timeline of Progress in Computer Chess

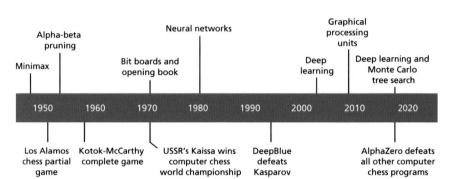

in architectures for deep learning and the advent of graphical processing units (GPUs), which made it feasible to train DNNs. While this new approach required immense numbers of simulated games for training, it proved capable of outperforming alpha-beta pruning in numerous games, including chess. In 2018, DeepMind's AlphaZero bested the most powerful previous chess engine, Stockfish, and an open-source DRL+MCTS chess engine, Leela Chess Zero, exceeded Stockfish's performance in mid-2019.[2]

The growth of capability and manner of progress is also evident in real-time video games like *StarCraft II* (Figure A.2). Early chess programs used a search algorithm specialized for two-player games (alpha-beta pruning) and heuristics developed specifically for chess. In contrast, *StarCraft II* research has leveraged domain-general learning mechanisms, which ultimately also produced the highest levels of play in computer chess.

Together, the history of development in computer chess and *StarCraft II* illustrates common sources of innovation in AI research:

1. *Hardware.* Neural network implementations on GPUs are essential to implement large architectures and to train on large data

---

[2]   Silver et al., 2018.

Figure A.2
Timeline of Progress in *StarCraft II*

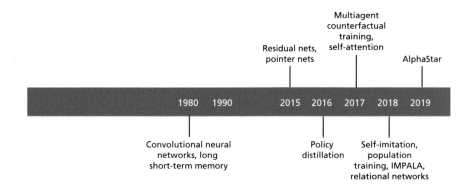

sets.[3] Additionally, the performance of computationally complex algorithms—for example, the minimax search algorithm—increases linearly with processing power.

2. *Algorithms and architectures.* Many algorithm advances are general. The discovery of techniques to address the problem of vanishing and exploding gradients enabled all manners of DNNs to be trained by gradient descent.[4] Other components in learning architectures—for example, convolutions, long short-term memory, and attention—have proven broadly useful. These components are now used in many different applications (e.g., computer vision, natural language processing, game play). Additionally, these components can be

---

[3]   K. S. Oh and K. Jung, "GPU Implementation of Neural Networks," *Pattern Recognition*, Vol. 37, No. 6, 2004; D. C. Ciresan, U. Meier, J. Masci, L. M. Gambardella, and J. Schmidhuber, "Flexible, High Performance Convolutional Neural Networks for Image Classification," *Proceedings of the Twenty-Second International Joint Conference on Artificial Intelligence*, Barcelona: AAAI Press, June 2011.

[4]   Sepp Hochreiter, Yoshua Bengio, Paolo Frasconi, and Jurgen Schmidhuber, "Gradient Flow in Recurrent Nets: The Difficulty of Learning Long-Term Dependencies," in John F. Kolen and Stefan C. Kremer, eds., *A Field Guide to Dynamical Recurrent Neural Networks*, Hoboken, N.J.: Wiley-IEEE Press, 2001.

combined into a single end-to-end system, as with DeepMind's AlphaStar.[5]

3. *Software toolboxes.* The need for open-source software implementations of neural networks to foster collaboration among researchers was recognized early on.[6] Popular software frameworks such as TensorFlow and PyTorch provide optimized implementations, which allow researchers to experiment with larger, more complex architectures.

4. *Data availability.* DNNs typically contain millions of tunable parameters and hence require large amounts of training data. The growth of the internet, the deployment of large database systems, crowdsourcing platforms, and the development of high-fidelity simulators have increased the availability of large data sets required to train DNNs.

---

[5]   Oriol Vinyals, Igor Babuschkin, Wojciech M. Czarnecki, Michaël Mathieu, Andrew Dudzik, Junyoung Chung, David H. Choi, Richard Powell, Timo Ewalds, Petko Georgiev et al., "Grandmaster Level in Starcraft II Using Multi-Agent Reinforcement Learning," *Nature*, Vol. 575, No. 7782, 2019.

[6]   Sören Sonnenburg, Mikio L. Braun, Cheng Soon Ong, Samy Bengio, Leon Bottou, Geoffrey Holmes, Yann LeCun, Klaus Robert Müller, Fernando Pereira, Carl Edward Rasmussen et al., "The Need for Open Source Software in Machine Learning," *Journal of Machine Learning Research*, Vol. 8, October 2007.

Mathematical Details for Closed-Loop Automatic Target Recognition

Closed-Loop Automatic Target Recognition

Defining x_t as the belief (confidence) at time t in the target class, the algorithm from Ssu-Hsin Yu and his colleagues' work proceeds as follows:[1]

1. Propagation of state x from time t to time $t + 1$ according to

$$P(x_{t+1}|a, a_{1...t}, y_{1...t}) = \sum_{t}^{x} P(x_{t+1}|a, x_t)P(x_t|a_{1...t}, y_{1...t}), \quad (1)$$

    where a is a candidate action to be taken, and $a_{1...t}$ and $y_{1...t}$ represent actions and observations up to time t.

2. Prediction of the next observation based on the candidate action a:

$$P(y_{t+1}|a, a_{1...t}, y_{1...t}) = \sum_{t+1}^{x} P(y_{t+1}|a, x_{t+1})P(x_{t+1}|a, a_{1...t}, y_{1...t}), \quad (2)$$

    where predictions are based on the confusion matrices and state information at time $t + 1$. The observation probabilities, $P(y_{t+1}|a, x_{t+1})$, are read in as rows in the confusion matrices.

---

[1]   Yu et al., 2015.

3. Calculation of the expected reward for candidate action a, $E(R(a)|a_{1...t}, y_{1...t})$, following

$$E(R(a)|a_{1...t}, y_{1...t}) = \sum_{t+1}^{y} (R(a)P(y_{t+1}|a, a_{1...t}, y_{1...t}), \qquad (3)$$

where $R(a) = -\sum_{x_{t+1}} P(x_{t+1}|a, a_{1...t}, y_{1...t+1}) \ln P(x_{t+1}|a, a_{1...t}, y_{1...t+1})$ and $P(x_{t+1}|a, a_{1...t}, y_{1...t+1}) \propto P(y_{t+1}|a, x_{t+1}) P(x_{t+1}|a, a_{1...t}, y_{1...t})$. $R(a)$ corresponds to the entropy of x_{t+1} conditional on all actions and observations up to time t.

4. The action with the highest expected reward is selected.

5. The posterior probability of the class confidence is then updated with the new observation y_{t+1}:

$$P(x_{t+1}|a_{1...t+1}, y_{1...t+1}) \propto P(y_{t+1}|a_{t+1}, x_{t+1}) \sum_{t}^{x} P(x_{t+1}|a_{t+1}, x_t) P(x_t|a_{1...t}, y_{1...t}). \quad (4)$$

The resulting coefficients are then normalized to 1.

Asynchronous Advantage Actor-Critic

An A3C agent learns by interacting with an environment and attempting to optimize its loss function, which can be broken down into three distinct elements: a policy loss, a value loss, and an entropy loss. The policy loss, $\pounds_\pi = \log \pi (a_t|s_t) A(s_t, a_t; \theta, \theta_v)$, is dependent on the policy performing an action a_2 in the state s_t at time step t, multiplied by the advantage $A(s_t, a_t; \theta, \theta_v)$, with policy parameters θ, θ' and value estimator parameters θ_v. The critics loss, $\pounds_v = (R_t - V(s_t; \theta'_v))^2$, is simply the mean squared error between R_t, which is the accumulated return as discounted by some factor γ and $V(s_t; \theta'_v)$, which is the critic estimate of the value. To promote exploration of the agent's decisions, we also include an entropy regularization term $H(\pi(s_t; \theta'))$. When we combine these terms, our loss function for optimizing becomes

$$\pounds_{tot} = \pounds_\pi + \alpha\pounds_v - \beta H, \qquad (5)$$

Table B.1
Asynchronous Advantage Actor-Critic
Hyperparameters

Parameter	Value
γ (discount)	0.99
Learning rate	5×10^{-4}
α	0.5
β	10^{-4}

which includes a scaling factor of α that can be used to reduce the potential for early convergence by the critic and β, which sets the contribution from entropy regularization.

The parameters used for training the A3C algorithm across all cases in this analysis are shown in Table B.1.

Modified *StarCraft II* Environment

In this technical case study, we used the *StarCraft II* Python API provided by DeepMind called Py *StarCraft II*. We developed a new method for scoring target observation and classification to modify the default environment. This method considers the total time spent observing a target, while rewarding exploration of other targets after reaching a critical duration. For example, the system gives the agent a reward of +1 once it correctly classifies a target (friend or foe) for five consecutive time steps and an addition reward of +1 for every correct consecutive classification thereafter. Once the agent has tracked a single target for ten consecutive time steps, a larger reward becomes available for switching to and tracking the second target. Formally, the scoring-penalty system is defined as

$$R = \begin{cases} +1, & \text{if } 1^{\text{st}} \text{ target, for TOS} \leq 10 \\ +1.1, & n^{\text{th}} \text{ target, } n \geq 2, \text{ for TOS} \leq 10 \\ -0.1, & \text{otherwise.} \end{cases} \qquad (6)$$

References

Arbel, T., and F. P. Ferrie, "On the Sequential Accumulation of Evidence," *International Journal of Computer Vision*, Vol. 43, 2001, pp. 205–230.

Ballard, Dana H., "Animate Vision," *Artificial Intelligence*, Vol. 48, No. 1, 1991, pp. 57–86.

Bandres, Wilmer, Blai Bonet, and Hector Geffner, "Planning with Pixels in (Almost) Real Time," *Thirty-Second AAAI Conference on Artificial Intelligence*, Palo Alto, Calif: AAAI Press, April 2018, pp. 6102–6109.

Ciresan, D. C., U. Meier, J. Masci, L. M. Gambardella, and J. Schmidhuber, "Flexible, High Performance Convolutional Neural Networks for Image Classification," *Proceedings of the Twenty-Second International Joint Conference on Artificial Intelligence*, Barcelona: AAAI Press, June 2011, pp. 1237–1242.

Crandall, B., G. Klein, and R. R. Hoffman, *Working Minds: A Practitioner's Guide to Cognitive Task Analysis*, Cambridge, Mass.: MIT Press, 2006.

Defense Innovation Board, *AI Principles: Recommendations on the Ethical Use of Artificial Intelligence by the Department of Defense*, Arlington, Va., 2019.

Defense Science Board, *Summer Study on Autonomy*, Washington, D.C.: Office of the Under Secretary of Defense, June 2016.

DoD—*See* U.S. Department of Defense.

Doubleday, Justin, "Pentagon Reviewing Policy on Autonomy in Weapon Systems amid Advances in Artificial Intelligence," *Inside Defense*, February 28, 2020. As of March 25, 2020:
https://insidedefense.com/daily-news/pentagon-reviewing-policy-autonomy
-weapon-systems-amid-advances-artificial-intelligence

Du, Zhengjun, Chao Chen, and Defeng Kong, "Modeling and Development of Course of Action by Considering Uncertainty and Antagonism," *Military Operations Research*, Vol. 19, No. 2, 2014, pp. 35–58.

Hochreiter, Sepp, Yoshua Bengio, Paolo Frasconi, and Jurgen Schmidhuber, "Gradient Flow in Recurrent Nets: The Difficulty of Learning Long-Term Dependencies," in John F. Kolen and Stefan C. Kremer, eds., *A Field Guide to Dynamical Recurrent Neural Networks*, Hoboken, N.J.: Wiley-IEEE Press, 2001, pp. 237–243.

Hoffman, Robert R., Beth Crandall, and Nigel Shadbolt. "Use of the Critical Decision Method to Elicit Expert Knowledge: A Case Study in the Methodology of Cognitive Task Analysis," *Human Factors*, Vol. 40, No. 2, 1998, pp. 254–276.

Joint Publication 5-0, *Joint Operation Planning*, Washington, D.C.: U.S. Joint Chiefs of Staff, 2017.

Khodyakov, D., S. Grant, B. Denger, K. Kinnett, A. Martin, M. Booth, C. Armstrong, E. Dao, C. Chen, I. Coulter, H. Peay, G. Hazlewood, and N. Street, "Using an Online, Modified Delphi Approach to Engage Patients and Caregivers in Determining the Patient-Centeredness of Duchenne Muscular Dystrophy Care Considerations," *Medical Decision Making*, Vol. 39, No. 8, 2019, pp. 1019–1031.

Koenig, Sven, and Reid G. Simmons, *Complexity Analysis of Real-Time Reinforcement Learning*, Pittsburgh, Pa.: School of Computer Science Carnegie Mellon University, 1993, pp. 99–107.

Lipovetzky, Nir, and Hector Geffner, "Width and Serialization of Classical Planning Problems," *ECAI '12: Proceedings of the 20th European Conference on Artificial Intelligence*, Amsterdam: IOS Press, August 2012, pp. 540–545.

Mnih, V., A. P. Badia, M. Mirza, A. Graves, T. Lillicrap, T. Harley, D. Silver, and K. Kavukcuoglu, "Asynchronous Methods for Deep Reinforcement Learning," *Proceedings of the 33rd International Conference on Machine Learning*, Vol. 48, 2016, pp. 1928–1937.

Mnih, Volodymyr, Koray Kavukcuoglu, David Silver, Alex Graves, Ioannis Antonoglou, Daan Wierstra, and Martin Riedmiller, *Playing Atari with Deep Reinforcement Learning*, Ithaca, N.Y.: Cornell University, 2013.

National Science and Technology Council Committee on Science and Technology Enterprise, *Federal Cybersecurity Research and Development Strategic Plan*, Washington, D.C.: Executive Office of the President of the United States, 2019.

National Science and Technology Council Committee on Technology, *Preparing for the Future of Artificial Intelligence*, Washington, D.C.: Executive Office of the President, October 2016.

National Security Commission on Artificial Intelligence, *Interim Report*, Arlington, Va., 2019.

North Atlantic Treaty Organization, *Code of Best Practice for C2 Assessment*, Brussels: Research and Technology Organization, 2002.

NSTC—*See* National Science and Technology Council.

Oh, K. S., and K. Jung, "GPU Implementation of Neural Networks," *Pattern Recognition*, Vol. 37, No. 6, 2004, pp. 1311–1314.

Pendrith, Mark, *On Reinforcement Learning of Control Actions in Noisy and Non-Markovian Domains*, University of New South Wales, Sydney, UNSW-CSE TR-9410, 1994.

Rasmusen, E., *Games and Information: An Introduction to Game Theory*, Oxford: Blackwell, 1989.

Rosen, Julie A., and Wayne L. Smith, "Influence Net Modeling with Causal Strengths: An Evolutionary Approach," *Military Operations Research Society*, Vol. 33, No. 4, December 2000, pp. 6–7, 37–39.

Rossillon, Kevin. J., *Optimized Air Asset Scheduling Within a Joint Aerospace Operations Center*, Cambridge, Mass.: MIT Press, 2015.

Russell, S., and P. Norvig, *Introduction to Artificial Intelligence: A Modern Approach*, New Delhi: Prentice-Hall of India, 1995.

Select Committee on Artificial Intelligence, *The National Artificial Intelligence Research and Development Strategic Plan: 2019 Update*, Washington, D.C.: National Science and Technology Council, June 2019.

Shanahan, John, "Artificial Intelligence Initiatives," statement to the Senate Armed Services Committee Subcommittee on Emerging Threats and Capabilities, Washington, D.C., U.S. Senate, March 12, 2019.

Shannon, C. E., "Programming a Computer for Playing Chess," *Philosophical Magazine*, Vol. 41, 1950, pp. 256–275.

Silver, David, Thomas Hubert, Julian Schrittwieser, Ioannis Antonoglou, Matthew Lai, Arthur Guez, Marc Lanctot, Laurent Sifre, Dharshan Kumaran, Thore Graepel, Timothy Lillicrap, Karen Simonyan, and Demis Hassabi, "A General Reinforcement Learning Algorithm that Masters Chess, Shogi, and Go Through Self-Play," *Science*, Vol. 362, No. 6419, December 2018, pp. 1–32. As of March 23, 2020:
https://science.sciencemag.org/content/362/6419/1140

Sonnenburg, Sören, Mikio L. Braun, Cheng Soon Ong, Samy Bengio, Leon Bottou, Geoffrey Holmes, Yann LeCun, Klaus Robert Müller, Fernando Pereira, Carl Edward Rasmussen, Gunnar Ratsch, Bernhard Scholkopf, Alexander Smola, Pascal Vincent, Jason Weston, and Robert C. Williamson, "The Need for Open Source Software in Machine Learning," *Journal of Machine Learning Research*, Vol. 8, October 2007, pp. 2443–2466.

U.S. Air Force, *Operational Employment: Air Operations Center*, AFTTP 3-3 AOC, Washington, D.C., March 31, 2016. Not available to the general public.

U.S. Air Force Doctrine, Annex 3-30, *Command and Control*, Maxwell Air Force Base, Ala.: Lemay Center for Doctrine, 2020a.

————, Annex 3-50, *Personnel Recovery*, Maxwell Air Force Base, Ala.: Lemay Center for Doctrine, 2020b.

————, "Appendix D: Theater Air Control System," in *Annex 3-30: Command and Control*, Maxwell Air Force Base, Ala.: Lemay Center for Doctrine, 2020c.

U.S. Air Force Scientific Advisory Board, *Technologies for Enabling Resilient Command and Control MDC2 Overview*, Washington, D.C., 2018.

U.S. Department of Defense, *Glossary of Defense Acquisition Acronyms and Terms*, Fort Belvoir, Va.: Defense Acquisition University, 2017.

————, *Artificial Intelligence Strategy*, Washington, D.C., 2018.

Vinyals, Oriol, Igor Babuschkin, Wojciech M. Czarnecki, Michaël Mathieu, Andrew Dudzik, Junyoung Chung, David H. Choi, Richard Powell, Timo Ewalds, Petko Georgiev, Junhyuk Oh, Dan Horgan, Manuel Kroiss, Ivo Danihelka, Aja Huang, Laurent Sifre, Trevor Cai, John P. Agapiou, Max Jaderberg, Alexander S. Vezhnevets, Remi Leblond, Tobias Pohlen, Valentin Dalibard, David Budden, Yury Sulsky, James Molloy, Tom L. Paine, Caglar Gulcehre, Ziyu Wang, Tobias Pfaff, Yuhuai Wu, Roman Ring, Dani Yogatama, Dario Wunsch, Katrina McKinney, Oliver Smith, Tom Schaul, Timothy Lillicrap, Koray Kavukcuoglu, Demis Hassabis, Chris Apps, and David Silver, "Grandmaster Level in Starcraft II Using Multi-Agent Reinforcement Learning," *Nature*, Vol. 575, No. 7782, 2019, pp. 350–354.

Vinyals, Oriol, Timo Ewalds, Sergey Bartunov, Petko Georgiev, Alexander Sasha Vezhnevets, Michelle Yeo, Alireza Makhzani, Heinrich Küttler, John Agapiou, Julian Schrittwieser, John Quan, Stephen Gaffney, Stig Petersen, Karen Simonyan, Tom Schaul, Hado van Hasselt, David Silver, Timothy Lillicrap, Kevin Calderone, Paul Keet, Anthony Brunasso, David Lawrence, Anders Ekermo, Jacob Repp, and Rodney Tsing, "StarCraft II: A New Challenge for Reinforcement Learning," Ithaca, N.Y.: Cornell University, eprint arxiv:1708.04782, August 2017. As of December 30, 2020:
https://arxiv.org/abs/1708.04782

Yu, Ssu-Hsin, Pat McLaughlin, Aleksandar Zatezalo, Kai-yuh Hsiao, and J. Boskovic, "Integrate Knowledge Acquisition with Target Recognition Through Closed-Loop ATR," *Proceedings of Signal Processing, Sensor/Information Fusion, and Target Recognition XXIV*, Vol. 9474, 2015, pp. 1–12.

Zacharias, G., *Autonomous Horizons: The Way Forward*, Maxwell Air Force Base, Ala.: Air University Press, Curtis E. LeMay Center for Doctrine Development and Education, 2019.

Zaidi, Abbas K., Faisal Mansoor, and Titsa P. Papantoni-Kazakos, "Theory of Influence Networks," *Journal of Intelligent and Robotic Systems*, Vol. 60, No. 3–4, 2010, pp. 457–491.